To Papa

A Collection of Letters between Thomas Jefferson, and his daughter Martha

Dedicated to,
Those that love History

To Papa, To Patsy
1

Introduction

Author of the Declaration of Independence, Statesman, President, and Father. Thomas Jefferson was born in 1743 Albemarle County, Virginia.[1] He was the third born out of ten children, and the son of Peter and Jane Randolph Jefferson.

Thomas's father was a member of the Virginia House of Burgesses, a Judge, and a frontiersman.

When Thomas was fourteen years old in 1757, his father abruptly died. Thomas inherited approximately 7,500 acres of land, 21 horses and 53 slaves.

At the age of sixteen, Thomas applied to be admitted into the college of Willam and Mary, in Williamsburg, Virginia.[2] At the college, young Thomas studied the law.[3]

After college during the year 1770, his family's old home burned down, along with most of Thomas's books and other papers. Then in October he visited a wealthy lawyer named John Wayles.

Mr. Wayles had a widowed daughter with an infant son. Thomas took a liking to her and became her suitor. They married on New Years day, January 1, 1772.

---

[1] Thomas Jefferson. (n.d.). Retrieved from https://www.whitehouse.gov/about-the-white-house/presidents/thomas-jefferson/?utm_source=link

[2] Thomas Jefferson Biography. (n.d.). Retrieved from https://www.nps.gov/jeff/learn/historyculture/thomas-jefferson-biography.htm

[3] Thomas Jefferson. (n.d.). Retrieved from https://www.whitehouse.gov/about-the-white-house/presidents/thomas-jefferson/?utm_source=link

Over the course of the next ten years they would have a total of six children, but only two would survive to adulthood. The eldest was their daughter Martha, whom Thomas nicknamed, Patsy.[4]

Thomas was a member of the Second Continental Congress, and at the ripe age of 33, he drafted the Declaration Of Independence. In the years that followed he would work diligently in his home State of Virginia, but in 1785, he succeeded Benjamin Franklin as the Minister to France. Then after the second Constitution of the United States was established, he would serve as the first Secretary of State during the Washington administration. During his time as Secretary of State, he struck up a rivalry with the Secretary of Treasury, Alexander Hamilton. Thomas would resign his position in 1793.

Thomas ended up running reluctantly in the 1796 election against John Adams. Thomas lost by three votes, and because of how the Constitution was established at the time, Thomas became the Vice President.

Thomas would run again in the 1800 election, but he would gain victory this time.[5] He was sworn in as President of the United States of America on March 4, 1801.

***

During all this time, Thomas Jefferson kept writing to his daughter Martha or as he would call her, Patsy. The purpose of this collection is to show the more human side of Thomas Jefferson. We know him as the Politician, but by reading the letters Patsy and Thomas wrote each other,

[4] Thomas Jefferson Biography. (n.d.). Retrieved from https://www.nps.gov/jeff/learn/historyculture/thomas-jefferson-biography.htm

[5] Thomas Jefferson. (n.d.). Retrieved from https://www.whitehouse.gov/about-the-white-house/presidents/thomas-jefferson/?utm_source=link

you will be able to see Thomas Jefferson, the Man, and Thomas Jefferson the Father.

This collection covers four different periods. The first is before the Constitution, the second is during his time as Secretary of State, the third is during his time as Vice President, and the fourth is during his first term as President.

This collection is incomplete, and contains Thomas's and Patsy's spelling and grammar mistakes.

The goal of this collection is to get to know Thomas Jefferson better through his correspondence with Patsy, and this will hopefully be demonstrated with over 100 letters that were arranged in this collection.

At the beginning of each section, a brief summary of where both Patsy and Thomas Jefferson were in their lives will be given.

***

Without further ado, I present to you,

To Papa, To Patsy

A Collection Of Letters Between Thomas Jefferson,
And His Daughter Martha

Before The Constitution

1783 - 1788

Patsy was born on September 27, 1772, and by the time the first letter in this collection was written, she was eleven years old. By the last letter dated in this section Patsy would have been fifteen years old.

During this time Thomas Jefferson was involved with the State of Virginia, working on legislation. In 1785 he took over for Benjamin Franklin as the Minister to France, and his daughters Patsy and Polly came along with him.

Patsy would attend school in France while her Father was working as the Minister.

Thomas Jefferson would serve as the Minister to France until 1789, thus returning back to the United States with his daughters.

***

Without further ado,
The letters of Thomas and Patsy,
Before The Constitution

My dear Patsy

After four days journey I arrived here without any accident and in as good health as when I left Philadelphia. The conviction that you would be more improved in the situation I have placed you than if still with me, has solaced me on my parting with you, which my love for you has rendered a difficult thing. The acquirements which I hope you will make under the tutors I have provided for you will render you more worthy of my love, and if they cannot increase it they will prevent it's diminution. Consider the good lady who has taken you under her roof, who has undertaken to see that you perform all your exercises, and to admonish you in all those wanderings from what is right or what is clever to which your inexperience would expose you, consider her I say as your mother, as the only person to whom, since the loss with which heaven has been pleased to afflict you, you can now look up; and that her displeasure or disapprobation on any occasion will be an immense misfortune which should you be so unhappy as to incur by any unguarded act, think no concession too much to regain her good will. With respect to the distribution of your time the following is what I should approve.

from 8. to 10 o'clock practise music.

from 10. to 1. dance one day and draw another

from 1. to 2. draw on the day you dance, and write a letter the next day.

from 3. to 4. read French.

from 4. to 5. exercise yourself in music.

from 5. till bedtime read English, write &c.

Communicate this plan to Mrs. Hopkinson and if she approves of it pursue it. As long as Mrs. Trist remains in Philadelphia cultivate her affections. She has been a valuable friend to you and her good sense and good heart make her valued by all who know her and by nobody on earth more than by me. I expect you will write to me by every post. Inform me what books you read, what tunes you learn, and inclose me your best copy of every lesson in drawing. Write also one letter every week either to your aunt Eppes, your aunt Skipwith, your aunt Carr, or the little lady from whom I now inclose a letter, and always put the letter you so write under cover to me. Take care that you never spell a word wrong. Always before you write a word consider how it is spelt, and if you do not remember it, turn to a dictionary. It produces great praise to a lady to spell well. I have placed my happiness on seeing you good and accomplished, and no distress which this world can now bring on me could equal that of your disappointing my hopes. If you love me then, strive to be good under every situation and to all living creatures, and to acquire those accomplishments which I have put in your power, and which will go far towards ensuring you the warmest love of your affectionate father,

Th: Jefferson

P.S. keep my letters and read them at times that you may always have present in your mind those things which will endear you to me.[6]

---

[6] "From Thomas Jefferson to Martha Jefferson, 28 November 1783," *Founders Online,* National Archives, last modified June 13, 2018, http://founders.archives.gov/documents/Jefferson/01-06-02-0286.

My Dear Patsy

I wrote you by the post this day fortnight, since which I have received two letters from you. I am afraid that you may not have sent to the post office and therefore that my letter may be still lying there. Tho' my business here may not let me write to you every week yet it will not be amiss for you to enquire at the office every week. I wrote to Mr. House by the last post. Perhaps his letter may still be in the office. I hope you will have good sense enough to disregard those foolish predictions that the world is to be at an end soon. The almighty has never made known to any body at what time he created it, nor will he tell any body when he means to put an end to it, if ever he means to do it. As to preparations for that event, the best way is for you to be always prepared for it. The only way to be so is never to do nor say a bad thing. If ever you are about to say any thing amiss or to do any thing wrong, consider before hand. You will feel something within you which will tell you it is wrong and ought not to be said or done: this is your conscience, and be sure to obey it. Our maker has given us all, this faithful internal Monitor, and if you always obey it, you will always be prepared for the end of the world: or for a much more certain event which is death. This must happen to all: it puts an end to the world as to us, and the way to be ready for it is never to do a wrong act. I am glad you are proceeding regularly under your tutors. You must not let the sickness of your French master interrupt your reading French, because you are able to do that with the help of your dictionary. Remember I desired you to send me the best copy you should make of every lesson Mr. Cimitiere should set you. In this I hope you will be punctual, because it will let me see how you are going on. Always let me know too what tunes you play. Present my compliments to Mrs. Hopkinson, Mrs. House and Mrs. Trist. I had a letter from your uncle Eppes last week informing me that Polly is very well, and Lucy recovered from an indisposition. I am my dear Patsy Your affectionate father,

Th: Jefferson[7]

---

[7] "From Thomas Jefferson to Martha Jefferson, 11 December 1783," *Founders Online,* National Archives, last modified June 13, 2018, http://founders.archives.gov/documents/Jefferson/01-06-02-0303.

My dear Patsy

I hoped before this to have received letters from you regularly and weekly by the post, and also to have had a letter to forward from you to one of your aunts as I desired in my letter of November 27th. I am afraid you do not comply with my desires expressed in that letter. Your not writing to me every week is one instance, and your having never sent me any of your copies of Mr. Simitiere's lessons is another. I shall be very much mortified and disappointed if you become inattentive to my wishes and particularly to the directions of that letter which I meant for your principal guide. I omitted in that to advise you on the subject of dress, which I know you are a little apt to neglect. I do not wish you to be gayly clothed at this time of life, but that what you wear should be fine of it's kind; but above all things, and at all times let your clothes be clean, whole, and properly put on. Do not fancy you must wear them till the dirt is visible to the eye. You will be the last who will be sensible of this. Some ladies think they may under the privileges of the dishabille be loose and negligent of their dress in the morning. But be you from the moment you rise till you go to bed as cleanly and properly dressed as at the hours of dinner or tea. A lady who has been seen as a sloven or slut in the morning, will never efface the impression she then made with all the dress and pageantry she can afterwards involve herself in. Nothing is so disgusting to our sex as a want of cleanliness and delicacy in yours. I hope therefore the moment you rise from bed, your first work will be to dress yourself in such a stile as that you may be seen by any gentleman without his being able to discover a pin amiss, or any other circumstance of neatness wanting.

By a letter from Mr. Short I learn that your sisters are well. I hope I shall soon receive a letter from you informing me you are so. I wrote a letter to Polly lately, which I supposed her aunt would read to her. I dare say it pleased her, as would a letter from you. I am sorry Mrs. Trist has determined to go at so inclement a season, as I fear she will suffer much more than she expects. Present my compliments to her and the good family there, as also very particularly to Mrs. Hopkinson whose health and happiness I have much at heart. I hope you are obedient and respectful to her in every circumstance and that your manners will be such as to engage her affections. I am my Dear Patsy Yours sincerely & affectionately,

Th: Jefferson[8]

---

[8] "From Thomas Jefferson to Martha Jefferson, 22 December 1783," *Founders Online,* National Archives, last modified June 13, 2018, http://founders.archives.gov/documents/Jefferson/01-06-02-0322.

My dear Patsy

Your letter by the post is not yet come to hand, that by Mr. Beresford I received this morning. Your long silence had induced me almost to suspect you had forgotten me and the more so as I had desired you to write to me every week. I am anxious to know what books you read, what tunes you can play, and to receive specimens of your drawing. With respect to your meeting Mr. Simitiere at Mr. Rittenhouse's, nothing could give me more pleasure than your being much with that worthy family wherein you will see the best examples of rational life and learn to esteem and copy them. But I should be very tender of obtruding you on the family as it might perhaps be not always convenient to them for you to be there at your hours of attending Mr. Simitiere. I can only say then that if it has been desired by Mr. and Mrs. Rittenhouse in such a way as that Mrs. Hopkinson shall be satisfied they will not consider it as inconvenient, I would have you thankfully accept it and conduct yourself with so much attention to the family as that they may never feel themselves incommoded by it. I hope Mrs. Hopkinson will be so good as to act for you in this matter with that delicacy and prudence of which she is so capable. I have so much at heart your learning to draw, and should be uneasy at your losing this opportunity which probably is your last. But I remind you to inclose me every week a copy of all your lessons in drawing that I may judge how you come on. I have had very ill health since I came here. I have been just able to attend my duty in the state house, but not to go out on any other occasion. I am however considerably better. Present my highest esteem to Mrs. Hopkinson and accept yourself assurances of the sincere love with which I am my dear Patsy, Yours affectionately,

Th: Jefferson[9]

---

[9] "From Thomas Jefferson to Martha Jefferson, 15 January 1784,"
Founders Online, National Archives, last modified June 13, 2018, http://
founders.archives.gov/documents/Jefferson/01-06-02-0358.

Dear Patsy

I have received two or three letters from you since I wrote last. Indeed my health has been so bad that I have been able scarcely to read, write or do any thing else. Your letters to your aunt and the others shall be forwarded. I hope you will continue to inclose to me every week one for some of your friends in Virginia. I am sorry Mr. Cimetiere cannot attend you, because it is probable you will never have another opportunity of learning to draw, and it is a pretty and pleasing accomplishment. With respect to the paiment of the guinea, I would wish him to receive it, because if there is to be a doubt between him and me, which of us acts rightly, I would chuse to remove it clearly off my own shoulders. You must thank Mrs. Hopkinson for me for the trouble she gave herself in this matter, from which she will be relieved by paying Mr. Cimetiere his demand. Perhaps when the season becomes milder he will consent to attend you. I am sorry your French master cannot be more punctual. I hope you nevertheless read French every day as I advised you. Your letter to me in French gave me great satisfaction and I wish you to exercise yourself in the same way frequently. Your sisters are well. I am in hopes the money I had placed in the bank subject to Mrs. Hopkinson's order had not yet failed. Lest it should have done so, inform her that I have now sent there a further supply. Deliver my most respectful compliments to her & be assured of the love with which I am My dear Patsy Your's affectionately,

Th: Jefferson[10]

---

[10] "From Thomas Jefferson to Martha Jefferson, 18 February 1784," *Founders Online,* National Archives, last modified June 13, 2018, http://founders.archives.gov/documents/Jefferson/01-06-02-0404.

Dear Patsy

It is now very long since I have had a letter from you. I hope you continue in good health, and attention to the several objects for which I placed you in Philadelphia. I take for granted you go on with your music and dancing, that when your French master can attend, you receive his instructions, and read by yourself when he cannot. Let me know what books you have read since I left you, and what tunes you can play. Have you been able to coax Cimetiere to continue? Letters by yesterday's post inform me your sisters are well. I inclose you a letter I received from Dear Polly. I send herewith Mr. Zane's present of the looking glass which I dare say he intended for you. Wait upon Mrs. House and let her know, if she should not have heard from Mrs. Trist lately, that we have received a letter from her by a gentleman immediately from Fort Pitt. She is very well and expects to leave that place about the first of April. Present me in the most friendly terms to your patroness Mrs. Hopkinson & be assured of the love with which I am Dr. Patsy Yours affectionately,

Th: Jefferson

Mr. Maury will deliver you this, who is lately from Virginia and is my particular friend.[11]

---

[11] "From Thomas Jefferson to Martha Jefferson, 19 March 1784," *Founders Online,* National Archives, last modified June 13, 2018, http://founders.archives.gov/documents/Jefferson/01-07-02-0041.

Annapolis Apr. 4. 1784.

My Dear Patsy

This will be handed you by Genl. Gates, who going to Philadelphia furnishes me with the opportunity of writing to you. I am again getting my health, and have some expectations of going to Philadelphia ere long; but of this am not certain. I have had no letters from Eppington since I wrote you last, and have not received one from you I think these two months. I wish to know what you read, what tunes you play, how you come on in your writing, whether you have been able to persuade Simetiere to continue, how you do, and how Mrs. Hopkinson does. These are articles of intelligence which will always be pleasing to me. Present my compliments respectfully to Mrs. Hopkinson, give her occasion always to be pleased with your grateful returns for the kind care she takes of you, and be assured of the love with which I am Dr. Patsy Yours affectionately,

Th: Jefferson[12]

---

[12] "From Thomas Jefferson to Martha Jefferson, 4 April 1784," *Founders Online,* National Archives, last modified June 13, 2018, http://founders.archives.gov/documents/Jefferson/01-07-02-0069.

My dear Patsy

I have not received a letter from you since early in February. This is far short of my injunctions to write once a week by post. I wish this for my own gratification as well as for your improvement. I received yesterday letters from Eppington by which I learn that the families there and at Hors du monde are well, and that your cousin Cary has a son. Lucy has been unwell during the winter but is got better. I am in hopes the approaching mild season will reestablish my health perfectly, in which case I shall probably take a trip to Philadelphia. I wish much to know what books you have read since I left you, and what tunes you can play. Present my compliments affectionately to Mrs. Hopkinson. I inclose you a letter which I suppose to be from your aunt Eppes. I am my dear Patsy Your's affectionately,

Th: Jefferson[13]

---

[13] "From Thomas Jefferson to Martha Jefferson, 17 April 1784," *Founders Online,* National Archives, last modified June 13, 2018, http://founders.archives.gov/documents/Jefferson/01-07-02-0104.

Paris Mar. 6. 1786.

My dear Patsy

I shall be absent so short a time that any letter you would write to me would hardly get to London before I should be coming away; and it is the more discouraging to write as they open all letters in the post office. Should however sickness or any other circumstance render a letter to me necessary, send it here to Mr. Short and he will direct and forward it. I shall defer engaging your drawing master till I return. I hope then to find you much advanced in your music. I need not tell you what pleasure it gives me to see you improve in every thing agreeable and useful. The more you learn the more I love you, and I rest the happiness of my life on seeing you beloved by all the world, which you will be sure to be if to a good heart you join those accomplishments so peculiarly pleasing in your sex. Adieu my dear child; lose no moment in improving your head, nor any opportunity of exercising your heart in benevolence. Yours affectionately,

Th: Jefferson[14]

---

[14] "From Thomas Jefferson to Martha Jefferson, 6 March 1786," *Founders Online,* National Archives, last modified June 13, 2018, http://founders.archives.gov/documents/Jefferson/01-09-02-0286.

Being disapointed in my expectation of receiving a letter from my dear papa, I have resolved to break so painful a silence by giving you an example that I hope you will follow, particularly as you know how much pleasure your letters give me. I hope your wrist is better and I am inclined to think that your voyage is rather for your pleasure than for your health. However I hope it will answer both purposes. I will now tell you how I go on with my masters. I have began a beautiful tune with balbastre, done a very pretty landskip with Pariseau, a little man playing on the violin, and began another beautiful landskape. I go on very slowly with my *tite live*, its being in such ancient italian that I can not read with out my master and very little with him even. As for the dansing master I intend to leave him off as soon as my month is finished. Tell me if you are still determined that I shall dine at the abesse's table. If you are I shall at the end of my quarter. The kings speach and that of the eveque de Narbone has been copied all over the convent. As for Monseur he rose up to speak but sat down again with out daring to open his lips. I know no news but supose Mr. Short will write you enough for him and me too. Mde. Thaubenen desires her compliments to you. Adieu my dear papa. I am afraid you will not be able to read my scrawl, but I have not the time of coppying it over again. Therefore I must beg your indulgence and assure of the tender affection of yours,

M Jefferson

Pray write often and long letters.[15]

15 "To Thomas Jefferson from Martha Jefferson, 8 [March] 1787," *Founders Online,* National Archives, last modified June 13, 2018, http://founders.archives.gov/documents/Jefferson/01-11-02-0215.

My Dear Papa

Though the knowledge of your health gave me the greatest pleasure, yet I own I was not a little disappointed in not receiving a letter from you. However, I console myself with the thought of having one very soon, as you promised to write to me every week. Until now you have not kept your word the least in the world, but I hope you will make up for your silence by writing me a fine, long letter by the first opportunity. *Titus Livius* puts me out of my wits. I can not read a word by myself, and I read of it very seldom with my master; however, I hope I shall soon be able to take it up again. All my other masters go on much the same—perhaps better. Every body here is very well, particularly Madame L'Abbesse, who has visited almost a quarter of the new building—a thing that she has not done for two or three years before now. I have not heard any thing of my harpsichord, and I am afraid it will not come before your arrival. They make every day some new history on the Assemblée des Notables. I will not tell you any, for fear of taking a trip to the Bastile for my pains, which I am by no means disposed to do at this moment. I go on pretty well with Thucydides, and hope I shall very soon finish it. I expect Mr. Short every instant for my letter, therefore I must leave you. Adieu, my dear papa; be assured you are never a moment absent from my thoughts, and believe me to be, your most affectionate child,

M. Jefferson[16]

---

[16] "To Thomas Jefferson from Martha Jefferson, 25 March 1787," *Founders Online,* National Archives, last modified June 13, 2018, http://founders.archives.gov/documents/Jefferson/01-11-02-0236.

I was happy, my dear Patsy, to receive, on my arrival here, your letter informing me of your health and occupations. I have not written to you sooner because I have been almost constantly on the road. My journey hitherto has been a very pleasing one. It was undertaken with the hope that the mineral waters of this place might restore strength to my wrist. Other considerations also concurred. Instruction, amusement, and abstraction from business, of which I had too much at Paris. I am glad to learn that you are employed in things new and good in your music and drawing. You know what have been my fears for some time past; that you do not employ yourself so closely as I could wish. You have promised me a more assiduous attention, and I have great confidence in what you promise. It is your future happiness which interests me, and nothing can contribute more to it (moral rectitude always excepted) than the contracting a habit of industry and activity. Of all the cankers of human happiness, none corrodes it with so silent, yet so baneful a tooth, as indolence. Body and mind both unemployed, our being becomes a burthen, and every object about us loathsome, even the dearest. Idleness begets ennui, ennui the hypochrondria, and that a diseased body. No laborious person was ever yet hysterical. Exercise and application produce order in our affairs, health of body, chearfulness of mind, and these make us precious to our friends. It is while we are young that the habit of industry is formed. If not then, it never is afterwards. The fortune of our lives therefore depends on employing well the short period of youth. If at any moment, my dear, you catch yourself in idleness, start from it as you would from the precipice of a gulph. You are not however to consider yourself as unemployed while taking exercise. That is necessary for your health, and health is the first of all objects. For this reason if you leave your dancing master for the summer, you must increase your other exercise. I do not like your saying that you are unable to read the antient print of your Livy, but with the aid of your master. We are always equal to what we undertake with resolution. A little degree of this will enable you to decypher your Livy. If you always lean on your master, you will never be able to proceed without him. It is a part of the American character to consider nothing as desperate; to surmount every difficulty by resolution and contrivance. In Europe there are shops for every want. It's inhabitants therefore have no idea that their wants can be furnished otherwise. Remote from all other aid, we are obliged to invent and to execute; to find means within ourselves, and not to lean on others. Consider therefore the conquering your Livy as an exercise in the habit of surmounting difficulties, a habit which will be necessary to you in the country where you are to live, and without which you will be thought a very helpless animal, and less esteemed. Music, drawing, books, invention and exercise will be so many resources to you against ennui. But there are others which to this object add that of utility. These are the needle, and domestic oeconomy. The latter you cannot learn here, but the former you may. In the country life of America there are many moments when a woman can have recourse to nothing but her needle for employment. In a dull company and in dull weather for instance. It is ill manners to read; it is ill manners to leave them; no cardplaying there among genteel people; that is abandoned to blackguards. The needle is then a valuable resource. Besides without knowing to use it herself, how can the mistress of a family direct the works of her servants? You ask me to write you long letters. I will do it my dear, on condition you will read them from time to time, and practice what they will inculcate. Their precepts will be dictated by experience, by a perfect knowlege of the situation in which you will be placed, and by the fondest love for you. This it is which makes me wish to see you more qualified than common. My expectations from you are high: yet not higher than you may attain. Industry and resolution are all that are wanting. No body in this world can make me so happy, or so miserable as you. Retirement from public life will ere long become necessary for me. To your sister and yourself I look to render the evening of my life serene and contented. It's morning has been clouded by loss after loss till I have nothing left but you. I do not doubt either your affection or dispositions. But great exertions are necessary, and you have little time left to make them. Be industrious then, my dear child. Think nothing unsurmountable by resolution and application, and you will be all that I wish you to be. You ask me if it is my desire you should dine at the abbess's table? It is. Propose it as such to Madame de Traubenheim with my respectful compliments and thanks for her care of you. Continue to love me with all the warmth with which you are beloved by, my dear Patsy, yours affectionately,

Th: Jefferson[17]

[17] "From Thomas Jefferson to Martha Jefferson, 28 March 1787," *Founders Online,* National Archives, last modified June 13, 2018, http://founders.archives.gov/documents/Jefferson/01-11-02-0244.

My dear Patsy

I received yesterday at Marseilles your letter of March 25. and I received it with pleasure because it announced to me that you were well. Experience learns us to be always anxious about the health of those whom we love. I have not been able to write to you so often as I expected, because I am generally on the road; and when I stop any where, I am occupied in seeing what is to be seen. It will be some time now, perhaps three weeks before I shall be able to write to you again. But this need not slacken your writing to me, because you have leisure, and your letters come regularly to me. I have received letters which inform me that our dear Polly will certainly come to us this summer. By the time I return it will be time to expect her. When she arrives, she will become a precious charge on your hands. The difference of your age, and your common loss of a mother, will put that office on you. Teach her above all things to be good: because without that we can neither be valued by others, nor set any value on ourselves. Teach her to be always true. No vice is so mean as the want of truth, and at the same time so useless. Teach her never to be angry. Anger only serves to torment ourselves, to divert others, and alienate their esteem. And teach her industry and application to useful pursuits. I will venture to assure you that if you inculcate this in her mind you will make her a happy being in herself, a most inestimable friend to you, and precious to all the world. In teaching her these dispositions of mind, you will be more fixed in them yourself, and render yourself dear to all your acquaintance. Practice them then, my dear, without ceasing. If ever you find yourself in difficulty and doubt how to extricate yourself, do what is right, and you will find it the easiest way of getting out of the difficulty. Do it for the additional incitement of increasing the happiness of him who loves you infinitely, and who is my dear Patsy your's affectionately,

Th: Jefferson[18]

[18] "From Thomas Jefferson to Martha Jefferson, 7 April 1787," *Founders Online,* National Archives, last modified June 13, 2018, http://founders.archives.gov/documents/Jefferson/01-11-02-0266.

My dear Papa

I am very glad that the beginning of your voyage has been so pleasing, and I hope that the rest will not be less so, as it is a great consolation for me, being deprived of the pleasure of seeing you, to know at least that you are happy. I hope your resolution of returning in the end of April is always the same. I do not doubt but what Mr. Short has written you word that my sister sets off with Fulwar Skipwith in the month of May, and she will be here in July. Then, indeed, shall I be the happiest of mortals; united to what I have the dearest in the world, nothing more will be requisite to render my happiness complete. I am not so industrious as you or I would wish, but I hope that in taking pains I very soon shall be. I have already begun to study more. I have not heard any news of my harpsichord; it will be really very disagreeable if it is not here before your arrival. I am learning a very pretty thing now, but it is very hard. I have drawn several little flowers, all alone, that the master even has not seen; indeed, he advised me to draw as much alone as possible, for that is of more use than all I could do with him. I shall take up my Livy, as you desire it. I shall begin it again, as I have lost the thread of the history. As for the hysterics, you may be quiet on that head, as I am not lazy enough to fear them. Mrs. Barett has wanted me out, but Mr. Short told her that you had forgotten to tell Madame L'Abbesse to let me go out with her. There was a gentleman, a few days ago, that killed himself because he thought that his wife did not love him. They had been married ten years. I believe that if every husband in Paris was to do as much, there would be nothing but widows left. I shall speak to Madame Thaubeneu about dining at the Abbess's table. As for needlework, the only kind that I could learn here would be embroidery, indeed netting also; but I could not do much of those in America, because of the impossibility of having proper silks; however, they will not be totally useless. You say your expectations for me are high, yet not higher

33

than I can attain. Then be assured, my dear papa, that you shall be satisfied in that, as well as in any thing else that lies in my power; for what I hold most precious is your satisfaction, indeed I should be miserable without it. You wrote me a long letter, as I asked you; however, it would have been much more so without so wide a margin. Adieu, my dear papa. Be assured of the tenderest affection of your loving daughter,

M. Jefferson

Pray answer me very soon—a long letter, without a margin. I will try to follow the advice they contain with the most scrupulous exactitude.[19]

---

[19] "To Thomas Jefferson from Martha Jefferson, 9 April 1787," *Founders Online,* National Archives, last modified June 13, 2018, http://founders.archives.gov/documents/Jefferson/01-11-02-0270.

Mu Dear Papa

I was very sorry to see by your letter To Mr. Short that your return would be put off, however I hope of not much, as you must be here for the arival of my sister. I wish I was my self all that you tell me to make her, however I will try to be as near like it as I can. I have another landskape since I wrote to you last and began another peice of music. I have not been able to do more having been confined some time to my bed with a violent head ake and a pain in my side which afterwards blistered up and made me suffer a great deal. But I am now much better. I have seen a phisician who has just drawn two of my companions out of a most dreadful situation which gave me a great deal of trust in him but the most disagreable is that I have been obliged to discontinue all my masters and am able now to take only some of them, those that are the least fatiguing. However I hope soon to take them all very soon. Mde. L'abesse has just had a fluxion de poitrine and has been at the last extremity but now is better. The *pays bas* have revolted against the emperor who is gone to Prussia to join with the empress and the venitians to war against the turcs. The plague is in spain. A virginia ship comming to spain met with a corser of the same strength. They fought And the battle lasted an hour and a quarter. The Americans gained and boarded the corser where they found chains that had been prepared for them. They took them and made use of them for the algerians them selves. They returned to virginia from whence they are to go back to algers to change the prisoners to which if the algerians will not consent the poor creatures will be sold as slaves. Good god have we not enough? I wish with all my soul that the poor negroes were all freed. It greives my heart when I think that these our fellow creatures should be treated so teribly as they are by many of our country men. A coach and six well shut up was seen to go to the bastille and the baron de Breteuil went two hours before to prepare an apartment. They supose it to be Mde. De Polignac and her sister, however no one knows. The king asked Mr. D'harcourt how much a year was necessary for the Dauphin. M. D'harcourt ter having looked over the accounts told two millions upon which the king could help expressing his astonishement because each of his daughters cost him nine, so Mde. de Polignac has pocketed the rest. Mr. Smith is at Paris. That is all the news I know. They told me a great deal more but I have forgot it. Adieu my dear papa believe me to be for life your most tender and affectionate child,

M Jefferson[20]

---

[20] "To Thomas Jefferson from Martha Jefferson, 3 May 1787," *Founders Online,* National Archives, last modified June 13, 2018, http://founders.archives.gov/documents/Jefferson/01-11-02-0316.

My dear Patsy

I got back to Aix the day before yesterday, and found there your letter of the 9th. of April, from which I presume you to be well tho' you do not say so. In order to exercise your geography I will give you a detail of my journey. You must therefore take your map and trace out the following places. Dijon, Lyons, Pont St. Esprit, Nismes, Arles, St. Remis, Aix, Marseilles, Toulon, Hieres, Frejus, Antibes, Nice, Col de Tende, Coni, Turin, Vercelli, Milan, Pavia, Tortona, Novi, Genoa, by sea to Albenga, by land to Monaco, Nice, Antibes, Frejus, Brignolles, Aix, and Marseille. The day after tomorrow I set out hence for Aix, Avignon, Pont du Gard, Nismes, Montpelier, Narbonne, along the Canal of Languedoc to Toulouse, Bourdeaux, Rochefort, Rochelle, Nantes, Lorient, Nantes, Tours, Orleans and Paris where I shall arrive about the middle of June, after having travelled something upwards of a thousand leagues. From Genoa to Aix was very fatiguing, the first two days having been at sea, and mortally sick, two more clambering the cliffs of the Appennine, sometimes on foot, sometimes on a mule according as the path was more or less difficult, and two others travelling thro' the night as well as day, without sleep. I am not yet rested, and shall therefore shortly give you rest by closing my letter, after mentioning that I have received a letter from your sister, which tho a year old, gave me great pleasure. I inclose it for your perusal, as I think it will be pleasing to you also. But take care of it, and return it to me when I shall get back to Paris, for trifling as it seems, it is precious to me. When I left Paris, I wrote to London to desire that your harpsichord might be sent during the months of April and May, so that I am in hopes it will arrive a little before I shall, and give me an opportunity of judging whether you have got the better of that want of industry which I had began to fear would be the rock on which you would split. Determine never to be idle. No person will have occasion to complain of the want of

37

time, who never loses any. It is wonderful how much may be done, if we are always doing. And that you may be always doing good, my dear, is the ardent prayer of yours affectionately,

Th: Jefferson[21]

[21] "From Thomas Jefferson to Martha Jefferson, 5 May 1787," *Founders Online,* National Archives, last modified June 13, 2018, http://founders.archives.gov/documents/Jefferson/01-11-02-0327.

I write to you, my dear Patsy, from the Canal of Languedoc, on which I am at present sailing, as I have been for a week past, cloudless skies above, limpid waters below, and on each hand a row of nightingales in full chorus. This delightful bird had given me a rich treat before at the fountain of Vaucluse. After visiting the tomb of Laura at Avignon, I went to see this fountain, a noble one of itself, and rendered for ever famous by the songs of Petrarch who lived near it. I arrived there somewhat fatigued, and sat down by the fountain to repose myself. It gushes, of the size of a river, from a secluded valley of the mountain, the ruins of Petrarch's chateau being perched on a rock 200 feet perpendicular above. To add to the enchantment of the scene, every tree and bush was filled with nightingales in full song. I think you told me you had not yet noticed this bird. As you have trees in the garden of the convent, there must be nightingales in them, and this is the season of their song. Endeavor, my dear, to make yourself acquainted with the music of this bird, that when you return to your own country you may be able to estimate it's merit in comparison with that of the mocking bird. The latter has the advantage of singing thro' a great part of the year, whereas the nightingale sings but 5. or 6. weeks in the spring, and a still shorter term and with a more feeble voice in the fall. I expect to be at Paris about the middle of next month. By that time we may begin to expect our dear Polly. It will be a circumstance of inexpressible comfort to me to have you both with me once more. The object most interesting to me for the residue of my life, will be to see you both developing daily those principles of virtue and goodness which will make you valuable to others and happy in yourselves, and acquiring those talents and that degree of science which will guard you at all times against ennui, the most dangerous poison of life. A mind always employed is always happy. This is the true secret, the grand recipe for felicity. The idle are the only wretched. In a world which furnishes so many emploiments which are useful, and so many which are amusing, it is our own fault if we ever know what ennui is, or if we are ever driven to the miserable resource of gaming, which corrupts our dispositions, and teaches us a habit of hostility against all mankind.—We are now entering the port of Toulouse, where I quit my bark; and of course must conclude my letter. Be good and be industrious, and you will be what I shall most love in this world. Adieu my dear child. Yours affectionately,

Th: Jefferson[22]

[22] "From Thomas Jefferson to Martha Jefferson, 21 May 1787," *Founders Online,* National Archives, last modified June 13, 2018, http://founders.archives.gov/documents/Jefferson/01-11-02-0350.

My dear Papa

I was very glad to see by your letter that you were on your return, and I hope that I shall very soon have the pleasure of seeing you. My sister's letter gave me a great deal of happiness. I wish she would write to me; but as I shall enjoy her presence very soon, it will make up for a neglect that I own gives me the greatest pain. I still remember enough of geography to know where the places marked in your letter are. I intend to copy over my extracts and learn them by heart. I have learnt several new pieces on the harpsichord, drawn five landscapes and three flowers, and hope to have done something more by the time you come. I go on pretty well with my history, and as for *Tite Live* I have begun it three or four times, and go on so slowly with it that I believe I never shall finish it. It was in vain that I took courage; it serves to little good in the execution of a thing almost impossible. I read a little of it with my master who tells me almost all the words, and, in fine, it makes me lose my time. I begin to have really great difficulty to write English; I wish I had some pretty letters to form my style. Pray tell me if it is certain that my sister comes in the month of July, because if it is, Madame de Taubenheim will keep a bed for her. My harpsichord is not come yet. Madame L'Abbesse is better, but she still keeps her bed. Madame de Taubenheim sends her compliments to you. Pray how does your arm go? I am very well now. Adieu, my dear papa; as I do not know any news, I must finish in assuring you of the sincerest affection of your loving child,

M. Jefferson[23]

---

23 "To Thomas Jefferson from Martha Jefferson, 27 May 1787," *Founders Online,* National Archives, last modified June 13, 2018, http://founders.archives.gov/documents/Jefferson/01-11-02-0366.

My dear Patsy

Your letter of May 3. came to me at this place. Since this I hear nothing from you; but I hope your health is reestablished. I have received letters from America as late as March assuring me that your sister shall be sent this summer. At that time however they did not know certainly by what occasion she could come. There was a hope of getting her under care of the French Consul and his lady, who thought of coming to France. The moment and place of her arrival therefore are still incertain. I forgot in my last letter to desire you to learn all your old tunes over again perfectly, that I may hear them on your harpsichord on it's arrival. I have no news of it however since I left Paris, tho' presume it will arrive immediately as I had ordered. Learn some slow movements of simple melody, for the Celestini stop, as it suits such only. I am just setting out for Lorient, and shall have the happiness of seeing you at Paris about the 12th. or 15th. of this month, and of assuring you in person of the sincere love of your's affectionately,

Th: Jefferson[24]

---

[24] "From Thomas Jefferson to Martha Jefferson, 1 June 1787," *Founders Online,* National Archives, last modified June 13, 2018, http://founders.archives.gov/documents/Jefferson/01-11-02-0374.

Paris June 14. 1787.

I send you, my dear Patsy, the 15 livres you desired. You propose this to me as an anticipation of five weeks allowance. But do you not see my dear how imprudent it is to lay out in one moment what should accomodate you for five weeks? That this is a departure from that rule which I wish to see you governed by, thro' your whole life, of never buying any thing which you have not money in your pocket to pay for? Be assured that it gives much more pain to the mind to be in debt, than to do without any article whatever which we may seem to want. The purchase you have made is one of those I am always ready to make for you, because it is my wish to see you dressed always cleanly and a little more than decently. But apply to me first for the money before you make a purchase, were it only to avoid breaking thro' your rule. Learn yourself the habit of adhering vigorously to the rules you lay down for yourself. I will come for you about eleven o'c lock on Saturday. Hurry the making your gown, and also your reding-cote. You will go with me some day next week to dine at the Marquis Fayette's. Adieu my dear daughter. Your's affectionately,

Th: Jefferson[25]

25 "From Thomas Jefferson to Martha Jefferson, 14 June 1787," *Founders Online,* National Archives, last modified June 13, 2018, http://founders.archives.gov/documents/Jefferson/01-11-02-0400.

Friday July 6.

I shall with the greatest pleasure, my dear Patsy, participate with you of the honour of Miss Annesley's company in our ride this afternoon. Assure her of my thankfulness for it as well as your own. The day being warm, I shall not be with you till between five and six o'clock. Adieu my Dear Your's affectionately,

Th: J.[26]

---

[26] "From Thomas Jefferson to Martha Jefferson, 6 July [1787]," *Founders Online,* National Archives, last modified June 13, 2018, http:// founders.archives.gov/documents/Jefferson/01-15-02-0616.

Monday June 16. 1788

Madame de Corney proposes, my Dear to carry you to the Opera tomorrow evening. I will therefore call for you precisely at five oclock. Be ready without fail before that hour. Know exactly at what hour they will shut your doors in the evening, and as you come down to the carriage see exactly what oclock it is by the Convent clock that we may not be deceived as to the time. Adieu. Yours' affectionately

Th. J

Kisses to Polly. She will keep your supper for you till you return tomorrow night.[27]

---

[27] "From Thomas Jefferson to Martha Jefferson, 16 June 1788," *Founders Online,* National Archives, last modified June 13, 2018, http:// founders.archives.gov/documents/Jefferson/01-27-02-0703.

Thomas Jefferson as Secretary of State

1790 - 1793

On March 22, 1790, Thomas Jefferson was sworn in as Secretary of State for the Washington Administration. He had a fierce rivalry with the Secretary of Treasury Alexander Hamilton. He would serve as Secretary of State until December 31, 1793.

During February of 1790, Patsy would marry her third cousin, Thomas Mann Randolph Jr. At the time Patsy was seventeen years old. Her Husband would enter politics, getting into the Virginia State Senate in 1793.

Patsy had her first child in 1791, a girl named Anne Cary Randolph. She had another child during 1792, this time a boy named Thomas Jefferson Randolph. These were the only children Patsy would have during her Father's time as Secretary of State.

***

Without further ado,
The letters of Thomas and Patsy,
During Thomas Jefferson as Secretary of State

New York April 4. 1790.

My dear daughter

I saw in Philadelphia your friends Mrs. Trist and Miss Rittenhouse. Both complained of your not writing. In Baltimore I enquired after Mrs. Buchanan and Miss Holliday. The latter is lately turned methodist, the former was married the evening I was there to a Mr. Turnbull of Petersburg in Virginia. Of course you will see her there. I find it difficult to procure a tolerable house here. It seems it is a practice to let all the houses the 1st. of February, and to enter into them the 1st. of May. Of course I was too late to engage one, at least in the Broadway, where all my business lies. I have taken an indifferent one nearly opposite Mrs. Elsworth's which may give me time to look about me and provide a better before the arrival of my furniture. I am anxious to hear from you, of your health, your occupations, where you are &c. Do not neglect your music. It will be a companion which will sweeten many hours of life to you. I assure you mine here is triste enough. Having had yourself and dear Poll to live with me so long, to exercise my affections and chear me in the intervals of business, I feel heavily the separation from you. It is a circumstance of consolation to know that you are happier; and to see a prospect of it's continuance in the prudence and even temper both of Mr. Randolph and yourself. Your new condition will call for abundance of little sacrifices. But they will be greatly overpaid by the measure of affection they will secure to you. The happiness of your life depends now on the continuing to please a single person. To this all other objects must be secondary; even your love to me, were it possible that that could ever be an obstacle. But this it can never be. Neither of you can ever have a more faithful friend than myself, nor one on whom you can count for more sacrifices. My own is become a secondary object to the happiness of you both. Cherish then for me, my dear child, the affection of your husband, and continue to love me as you have done, and to render my life a blessing

49

by the prospect it may hold up to me of seeing you happy. Kiss Maria for me if she is with you, and present me cordially to Mr. Randolph: assuring yourself of the constant & unchangeable love of Your's affectionately,

Th: Jefferson[28]

[28] "From Thomas Jefferson to Martha Jefferson Randolph, 4 April 1790," *Founders Online,* National Archives, last modified June 13, 2018, http://founders.archives.gov/documents/Jefferson/01-16-02-0172.

I recieved yours My Dearest Father with more pleasure than is possible for me to express and am happy to hear that you are at last settled at New Yorck as I am in hopes we shall now hear from you often. We are just returned from a visit up the country to aunt Carr and Mrs. Flemming's. It has not been possible as yet to carry dear Pol to Eppington for want of horses as Mr. Randolph was unwilling to borrow his father's for so long a time but I expect certainly to be there in ten days at latest. I intend writing to Mrs. Trist and Holly by the next post and promise you not to leave Richmond without writing also to my friends in Europe. I hope you have not given over comming to Virginia this fall as I assure you My dear papa my happiness can never be compleat without your company. Mr. Randolph omits nothing that can in the least contribute to it. I have made it my study to please him in every *thing* and do consider all other objects as secondary to that *except* my love for you. I do not know where we are to spend the summer. Mr. Randolph has some thought of settling at Varina for a little while till he can buy a part of Edgehill. I am much averse to it my self but shall certainly comply if he thinks it necessary. My health is perfectly good as also dear Polly's. I have recieved a letter from Mrs. Curson who informs me that the Duke of Dorset and Lady Caroline are both going to be married, the former to a Miss Cope. Adieu My Dear Pappa I am with the tenderest affection yours,

M. Randolph[29]

My dear Patsy

I wrote you last on the 4th. instant. In my letter of the 19th. to Mr. Randolph I inclosed one to you from England. I now send a packet from France, which comes from Botidour. I have now been seven weeks from you my dear and have never heard one tittle from you. I write regularly once a week to Mr. Randolph, yourself, or Polly, in hopes it may induce a letter from one of you every week also. If each would answer by the first post my letter to them, I should receive it within the three weeks so as to keep up a regular correspondence with each. I hope there are letters on the way for me. What I mentioned to Mr. Randolph in my letter of last week relative to Mr. Bedford is not confirmed. Some deny the fact. I inclose for Mr. Randolph Fenno's paper. He promises henceforward to give his foreign news from the Leyden gazette, so that it will be worth reading. I long to hear how you pass your time. I think both Mr. Randolph and yourself will suffer with ennui at Richmond. Interesting occupations are essential to happiness: indeed the whole art of being happy consists in the art of finding emploiment. I know none so interesting, and which croud upon us so much, as those of a domestic nature. I look forward therefore to your commencing housekeepers on your own farm, with some anxiety. Till then you will not know how to fill up your time, and your weariness of the things around you will assume the form of a weariness of one another. I hope Mr. Randolph's idea of settling near Monticello will gain strength; and that no other settlement will in the mean time be fixed on. I wish some expedient may be devised for settling him at Edgehill. No circumstance ever made me feel so strongly the thraldom of Mr. Wayles's debt. Were I liberated from that, I should not fear but that Colo. Randolph and myself, by making it a joint contribution, could effect the fixing you there, without interfering with what he otherwise proposes to give to Mr. Randolph. I shall hope when I return to Virginia in the fall that some means may be found of effecting all our wishes. Present me affectionately to Mr. Randolph and Polly, and my friendly respects to Colo. Randolph. Adieu my dear. Your's affectionately,

Th: Jefferson[30]

---

[30] "From Thomas Jefferson to Martha Jefferson Randolph, 26 April 1790," *Founders Online,* National Archives, last modified June 13, 2018, http://founders.archives.gov/documents/Jefferson/01-16-02-0220.

New York May 16. 1790.

My dear Patsy

Your's of the 25th. of April came to hand ten days ago, and yesterday I received Mr. Randolph's of the 3d. instant. When I wrote to him last week, I hoped to have been soon rid of the periodical headach which had attacked me. It has indeed been remarkeably slight since that, but I am not yet quite clear of it. I expect every fit to be the last. I inclose the newspapers for Mr. Randolph. He will probably judge, as the world does, from the stile and subject of the discourses on Davila, that they are the production of the Vice-president.—On Monday last the President was taken with a peripneumony, of threatening appearance. Yesterday (which was the 5th. day) he was thought by the physicians to be dying. However about 4. oclock in the evening a copious sweat came on, his expectoration, which had been thin and ichorous, began to assume a well digested form, his articulation became distinct, and in the course of two hours it was evident he had gone thro' a favorable crisis. He continues mending to-day, and from total despair we are now in good hopes of him. Indeed he is thought quite safe. My head does not permit me to add more than the affectionate love to you all of Yours,

Th: Jefferson[31]

---

[31] "From Thomas Jefferson to Martha Jefferson Randolph, 16 May 1790," *Founders Online,* National Archives, last modified June 13, 2018, http://founders.archives.gov/documents/Jefferson/01-16-02-0250.

New York June 6. 1790

My dear daughter

Your favor of May 28. from Eppington came to me yesterday, with the welcome which accompanies ever the tidings I recieve from you. Your resolution to go to housekeeping is a good one, tho' I think it had better be postponed till the fall. You are not yet seasoned to the climate, and it would therefore be prudent not to go to a sickly position till the sickly season is over. My former letters to Mr. Randolph and yourself will have apprised you of the pleasure it will give me to see you fixed in Albemarle; and the wish to co-operate in this, and to effect it, will determine me to come to Virginia in September or October at all events. Till then I should think it better that you should take no measures for Varina which might be inconvenient.—The lower house of Congress have voted to remove to Philadelphia. It is thought the Senate will be equally divided on the question, and consequently that the decision will rest with the Vice-President. Were we to be removed there, I should be so much nearer to you. I had an attack of my periodical head-ach, very violent for a few days. It soon subsided so as to be very slight. I am not quite clear of it now, tho I have been able to resume business for this week past. It can hardly be called a pain now, but only a disagreeable sensation of the head every morning. I am going tomorrow on a sailing party of three or four days with the President. Should we meet sea enough to make me sick I shall hope it will carry off the remains of my headach. Assure Mr. Randolph of my affectionate remembrance. I suppose Maria is not with you. Adieu my dear Daughter Your's affectionately,

Th: Jefferson[32]

---

[32] "From Thomas Jefferson to Martha Jefferson Randolph, 6 June 1790," *Founders Online,* National Archives, last modified June 13, 2018, http://founders.archives.gov/documents/Jefferson/01-16-02-0272.

My dear Martha

My last news from you were conveyed in your letter of May 28. I ascribe this to your present ambulatory life. I hope when you are more in the way of the post, I shall receive letters regularly once a week from one or other of you, as I write regularly once a week myself. In my letter of the last week to Mr. Randolph I mentioned the appearances of a war between England and Spain. We have nothing newer on that subject. There is a report indeed that there are three British frigates off our cost; but I know not on what it is founded. I think it probable that Congress will pass a bill for removing to Philadelphia for ten years, and then to Georgetown. The question will be brought on tomorrow, and it's fate be determined probably in the course of the ensuing week. I shall not be able to decide the time of my coming to Virginia till Congress shall have adjourned. The moment I can fix it I will inform you of it. I inclosed you the last week a letter from some of your English acquaintance. I now inclose you an engraving of the President done by Wright who drew the picture of him which I have at Paris. My tender affections attend you all. Adieu, my dear. Your's affectionately,

Th: Jefferson[33]

---

[33] "From Thomas Jefferson to Martha Jefferson Randolph, 27 June 1790," *Founders Online,* National Archives, last modified June 13, 2018, http://founders.archives.gov/documents/Jefferson/01-16-02-0340.

My dear Patsy

I recieved two days ago yours of July 2. with Mr. Randolph's of July 3. Mine of the 11th. to Mr. Randolph will have informed you that I expect to set out from hence for Monticello about the 1st. of September. As this depends on the adjournment of Congress and they begin to be impatient, it is more probable I may set out sooner than later. However my letters will keep you better informed as the time approaches.—Colo. Randolph's marriage was to be expected. All his amusements depending on society, he cannot live alone. The settlement spoken of may be liable to objections in point of prudence and justice. However I hope it will not be the cause of any diminution of affection between him and Mr. Randolph and yourself. That cannot remedy the evil, and may make it a great deal worse. Besides your interests which might be injured by a misunderstanding be assured that your happiness would be infinitely affected. It would be a cankerworm corroding eternally on your minds. Therefore, my dear child, redouble your assiduities to keep the affections of Colo. Randolph and his lady (if he is to have one) in proportion as the difficulties increase. He is an excellent good man, to whose temper nothing can be objected but too much facility, too much milk. Avail yourself of this softness then to obtain his attachment. If the lady has any thing difficult in her dispositions, avoid what is rough, and attach her good qualities to you. Consider what are otherwise as a bad stop in your harpsichord. Do not touch on it, but make yourself happy with the good ones. Every human being, my dear, must thus be viewed according to what it is good for, for none of us, no not one, is perfect; and were we to love none who had imperfections this world would be a desert for our love. All we can do is to make the best of our friends: love and cherish what is good in them, and keep out of the way of what is bad: but no more think of rejecting them for it than of throwing away a piece of music for a flat passage or two. Your situation will require peculiar attentions and respects to both parties. Let no proof be too much for either your patience or acquiescence. Be you, my dear, the link of love, union, and peace for the whole family. The world will give you the more credit for it in proportion to the difficulty of the task. And your own happiness will be the greater as you percieve that you promote that of others. Former acquaintance, and equality of age, will render it the easier for you to cultivate and gain the love of the lady. The mother too becomes a very necessary object of attentions.—This marriage renders it doubtful with me whether it will be better to direct our overtures to Colo. R. or Mr. H. for a farm for Mr. Randolph. Mr. H. has a good tract of land on the other side Edgehill, and it may not be unadviseable to begin by buying out a dangerous neighbor. I wish Mr. Randolph could have him sounded to see if he will sell, and at what price; but sounded thro' such a channel as would excite no suspicion that it comes from Mr. Randolph or myself. Colo. Monroe would be a good and unsuspected hand, as he once thought of buying the same lands. Adieu my dear child. Present my warm attachment to Mr. Randolph. Your's affectionately,

Th: Jefferson[34]

[34] "From Thomas Jefferson to Martha Jefferson Randolph, 17 July 1790," *Founders Online,* National Archives, last modified June 13, 2018, http://founders.archives.gov/documents/Jefferson/01-17-02-0023.

New York Aug. 8. 1790.

Congress being certainly to rise the day after tomorrow, I can now, my dear Patsy, be more certain of the time at which I can be at Monticello, and which I think will be from the 8th. to the 15th. of September: more likely to be sooner than later. I shall leave this about a fortnight hence, but must stay some days to have arrangements taken for my future residence in Philadelphia. I hope to be able to pass a month at least with you at Monticello. I am in hopes Mr. Randolph will take dear Poll in his pocket. Tell him I have sent him the model of the mould-board by Mr. David Randolph who left this place yesterday. I must trouble you to give notice to Martin to be at Monticello by the 1st. of September that he may have things prepared. If you know any thing of Bob, I should be glad of the same notice to him, tho' I suppose him to be in the neighborhood of Fredericksbg. and in that case I will have him notified thro' Mr. Fitzhugh. I have written to Mr. Brown for some necessaries to be sent to Monticello, and to send on some chairs which will go hence to the care of Mr. D. Randolph at the Hundred, to be forwarded to Mr. Brown at Richmond. If Mr. Randolph can give a little attention to the forwarding these articles we shall be the more comfortable. Present me to him and Maria affectionately, and continue to love me as I do you, my dear. Most sincerely,

Th: Jefferson[35]

[35] "From Thomas Jefferson to Martha Jefferson Randolph, 8 August 1790," *Founders Online,* National Archives, last modified June 13, 2018, http://founders.archives.gov/documents/Jefferson/01-17-02-0084.

New York Aug. 22. 1790.

My Dear Daughter

The last letter I recieved from you was of the 2d July. In mine of the 14th. inst. to Mr. Randolph I informed him I should set out the next day to Rhode island with the President. I did so, and returned yesterday, after a very pleasant sail of two days going and two days returning thro the Sound. We visited Newport and Providence, where the President was received with great cordiality. He expects to leave this place the 30th. My letter of about that date will inform Mr. Randolph of the day I shall set out from hence, which will probably be about the 1st. of Sep. and allowing for my necessary detention at Philadelphia, I shall in that case be at Monticello between the 14th. and 20th. of September, where I shall hope the pleasure of passing a month with you. I am afraid you will suffer inconvenience from the detention of your harness; but without it I could not have used my carriage till I recieve my own harness from France which I hardly expect now till September.-I think you understood Lady Caroline Tufton was about to be married. But in a London paper put into my hands by Mr. Rutledge I saw her attendance at court mentioned and under the name you knew her by.-We have no news yet whether the war between England and Spain has commenced. Kiss dear Poll for me, and remember me to Mr. Randolph. Adieu my dear. Your's affectionately,

Th: Jefferson[36]

[36] "From Thomas Jefferson to Martha Jefferson Randolph, 22 August 1790," *Founders Online,* National Archives, last modified June 13, 2018, http://founders.archives.gov/documents/Jefferson/01-17-02-0111.

Philadelphia Dec. 1. 1790.

My dear daughter

In my letter of last week to Mr. Randolph I mentioned that I should write every Wednesday to him, yourself and Polly alternately, and that my letters arriving at Monticello the Saturday and the answer being sent off on Sunday I should recieve it the day before I should have to write again to the same person, so as that the correspondence with each would be exactly kept up. I hope you will do it on your part. I delivered the fan and note to your friend Mrs. Waters (Miss Rittenhouse that was) she being now married to a Doctr. Waters. They live in the house with her father. She complained of the petit format of your letter, and Mrs. Trist of no letter. I inclose you the Magasin des modes of July.—My furniture is arrived from Paris: but it will be long before I can open the packages, as my house will not be ready to recieve them for some weeks. As soon as they are the mattrasses &c. shall be sent on.—News for Mr. Randolph. The letters from Paris inform that as yet all is safe there. They are emitting great sums of paper money. They rather believe there will be no war between Spain and England: but the letters from London count on a war, and it seems rather probable. A general peace is established in the North of Europe, except between Russia and Turkey. It is expected between them also. Wheat here is a French crown the bushel. Kiss dear Poll for me. Remember me to Mr. Randolph. I do not know yet how the Edgehill negociation has terminated. Adieu my dear, Your's affectionately,

Th: Jefferson[37]

---

[37] "From Thomas Jefferson to Martha Jefferson Randolph, 1 December 1790," *Founders Online,* National Archives, last modified June 13, 2018, http://founders.archives.gov/documents/Jefferson/01-18-02-0078.

Philadelphia Dec. 23. 1790.

My Dear Daughter

This is a scolding letter for you all. I have not recieved a scrip of a pen from home since I left it which is now eleven weeks. I think it so easy for you to write me one letter every week, which will be but once in three weeks for each of you, when I write one every week who have not one moment's repose from business from the first to the last moment of the week. Perhaps you think you have nothing to say to me. It is a great deal to say you are all well, or that one has a cold, another a fever &c., besides that there is not a sprig of grass that shoots uninteresting to me, nor any thing that moves, from yourself down to Bergere or Grizzle. Write then my dear daughter punctually on your day, and Mr. Randolph and Polly on theirs. I suspect you may have news to tell me of yourself of the most tender interest to me. Why silent then?

I am still without a house, and consequently without a place to open my furniture. This has prevented my sending you what I was to send for Monticello. In the mean time the river is frozen up so as that no vessel can get out, nor probably will these two months: so that you will be much longer without them than I had hoped. I know how inconvenient this will be and am distressed at it; but there is no help. I send a pamphlet for Mr. Randolph. My best affections to him, Polly, & yourself. Adieu my dear,

Th: Jefferson[38]

[38] "From Thomas Jefferson to Martha Jefferson Randolph, 23 December 1790," *Founders Online,* National Archives, last modified June 13, 2018, http://founders.archives.gov/documents/Jefferson/01-18-02-0127.

I very much regret not having answer'd yours My Dearest Papa sooner, but being misinformed with regard to the Charlottesville post which we heard was discontinued has till now prevented my writing and not as you supposed having nothing to say. It is unlucky that the matrasses can not be sent now as we shall soon be in great distress. Aunt Fleming and probably one of her sons being expected here shortly I must accept of Mrs. Lewis's kind offer who in returning one of the beds I sent home offered a second if necessary. I have reason to think my self far advanced in her good graces as she has really been friendly. Martin has left us and not relying much in the carefullness of the boys particularly when left to them selves I took an account of the plate china and locked up all that was not in imediate use. Not recollecting that there was a set of queens ware here I sent to Richmond for some by which means the china was preserved entire except our beautiful cups which being obliged to leave out are all broke but one. The spoons &c. that are in use are counted and locked up night and morning so that I hope to keep them all to gather till your return. It was very troublesome in the begining tho now I have the boys in tolerable order every thing goes on pretty well. I have wrought an entire reformation on the rest of my household. Nothing comes in or goes out without my knowledge and I believe there is as little waste as possible. I visit the kitchen smoke house and fowls when the weather permits and according to your desire saw the meat cut out. I can give but a poor account of my reading having had so little time to my self that tho I really have the greatest inclination I have not as yet been able to indulge it. Polly improves weekly in her spanish which she reads with much more facility than when you went away. She was surprised that I should think of making her look for *all* the words and the parts of the verb also when she made nonsence but finding me inexorable she is at last reconciled to her

63

dictionary with whom she had for some time past been on very bad terms. She has been twice thro her grammar since your departure. As for the harpsicord tho I put it in fine order it has been to little purpose till very lately. I am in hopes she will continue to attend to that also. She is remarkably docile where she can surmount her Laziness of which she has an astonishing degree and which makes her neglect what ever she thinks will not be imediately discovered. I have entered into all these details because however trifling they would appear to others, to you my Dear Papa I think they will be interesting. I received a kind invitation from Aunt Eppes to spend the month of February at Eppinton but Mrs. Fleming's being here at that time will render it useless. The morning of the 13th at 10 minutes past four we had an earthquake which was severe enough to awaken us all in the house and several of the servants in the out houses. It was followed by a second shock very slight and an aurora borealis. I am extremely obliged to you for the cypress vine which with a bundle of seeds I found in rumaging up some drawer in the chamber, written on the back *cupressus Patula* and some others. I intend to decorate my windows this spring. You promised me a colection of garden seeds for a young Lady in the west indies for whom also I will send you a letter to be forwarded to her with them. Adieu My Dearest Father. Mr. Randolph and Polly join in love. Believe me ever your affectionate child.

M. Randolph[39]

[39] "To Thomas Jefferson from Martha Jefferson Randolph, 16 January 1791," *Founders Online,* National Archives, last modified June 13, 2018, http://founders.archives.gov/documents/Jefferson/01-18-02-0173.

My Dear Daughter

Mr. Short in a late letter says that your acquaintances in Panthemont complain excessively of your inattention to them and desired him to mention it. Matters there are going on well. The sales of the church lands are succesful beyond all calculation. There has been a riot in Paris in which M. de Castrie's houshould furniture was destroyed. I am opening my things from Paris as fast as the workmen will make room for me. In a box lately opened I find a copy of the octavo edition of the Encyclopedie, and a complete copy of Buffon's works with Daubenton's part which I had written for to present to Mr. Randolph. But I do not know when I shall be able to send any thing forward from the slowness of workmen in making houseroom for me to open my things and for the ice in the river.—The cold of this place has made me wish for some stockings of cotton and hair's fur knit together. I do not recall whether Bet can knit. If she can do it well, it might be a good employment for her sometimes. If she cannot, I wish a good knitter could be found in the neighborhood to knit some for me. They should be very large. Present my cordial regards to Mr. Randolph, and kiss Polly for me, telling her I have received not a single letter from Monticello since I left it, except one from Mr. Randolph. Adieu my dear. Your's affectionately,

Th: Jefferson

P.S. The inclosed letter is for a neighbor of yours being somewhere on the waters of Buckisland. It is from her sister who is in Paris, the wife of one of the Duke of Orleans's grooms. He was of General Phillips's army.[40]

---

[40] "From Thomas Jefferson to Martha Jefferson Randolph, 20 January 1791," *Founders Online,* National Archives, last modified June 13, 2018, http://founders.archives.gov/documents/Jefferson/01-18-02-0187.

My dear Martha

I have this moment recieved yours of January 16. and answer it by the first post. It is indeed an interesting letter to me as it gives me details which I am sure will contribute to your happiness, my first wish. Nothing is so engaging as the little domestic cares into which you appear to be entering, and as to reading it is useful for only filling up the chinks of more useful and healthy occupations. I am sincerely sorry that the mattrasses cannot yet be forwarded. But the state of the river here forbids it, and while it is incertain whether it will be found open or shut no vessels come here from Virginia. They shall go by the first possible opportunity. Whenever your letter to Bruny comes I will accompany it with the seeds: but you must inform me at the same time what kind of seeds to send her.—Congress will certainly rise the 1st. of March, when you will again have Colo. Munroe and Mrs. Monroe in your neighborhood. I write to you out of turn, and believe I must adopt the rule of only writing when I am written to, in hopes that may provoke more frequent letters. Mr. Randolph's letter of Dec. 27. and your's now acknowledged are all I have recieved from Monticello since I left it. Give my best affections to him and Poll, and be assured my dear daughter of the sincere love of Yours affectionately,

Th: Jefferson[41]

41 "From Thomas Jefferson to Martha Jefferson Randolph, 2 February 1791," *Founders Online,* National Archives, last modified June 13, 2018, http://founders.archives.gov/documents/Jefferson/01-19-02-0017.

My dear Martha

Your two last letters are those which have given me the greatest pleasure of any I ever recieved from you. The one announced that you were become a notable housewife, the other a mother. This last is undoubtedly the key-stone of the arch of matrimonial happiness, as the first is it's daily aliment. Accept my sincere congratulations for yourself and Mr. Randolph. I hope you are getting well, towards which great care of yourself is necessary: for however adviseable it is for those in health to expose themselves freely, it is not so for the sick. You will be out in time to begin your garden, and that will tempt you to be out a great deal, than which nothing will tend more to give you health and strength. Remember me affectionately to Mr. Randolph and Polly, as well as to Miss Jenny. Your's sincereley,

Th: Jefferson[42]

---

[42] "From Thomas Jefferson to Martha Jefferson Randolph, 9 February 1791," *Founders Online,* National Archives, last modified June 13, 2018, http://founders.archives.gov/documents/Jefferson/01-19-02-0039.

Philadelphia Mar. 2.

My dear daughter

The present will serve just to tell you that I am well, and to keep up my plan of writing once a week whether I have any thing to say or not. Congress rises tomorrow. They have passed no laws remarkeable except the excise law and one establishing a bank. Mrs. Trist and Mrs. Waters always enquire after you and desire me to remember them to you. I hope you are by this time able to be about again and in good health as well as the little one. Kiss it and Maria for me. I have received her letter and will answer it next week. I inclose a letter for M. de Rieux. Present my esteem to Mr. Randolph.—Your's affectionately,

Th: Jefferson[43]

---

[43] "From Thomas Jefferson to Martha Jefferson Randolph, 2 March 1791," *Founders Online,* National Archives, last modified June 13, 2018, http://founders.archives.gov/documents/Jefferson/01-19-02-0096.

My Dear Papa

You gave us reason to hope in your last to Mr. Randolph that there was a probability of our seeing you this summer. Your little grand daughter thinks herself entitled to a visit. I hope you will not disapoint us. My house keeping and Polly's spanish have equally suffered from my confinement. She is beginning again to go on tolerably for so great a habit of idleness had she contracted in one month that it has taken another to get the better of it. I have at last seriously writing to my European friends tho I fear it will be a difficult tter to forward my letters to you as the post has ceased to go. Doctor Gilmer's eldest son is arrived from Scotland in a very deep consumption. His father and mother are gone down to Shirley in all probability to take their last farewell of him, if he is still alive which they almost dispaired of when they set off. A cousin of ours Randolph Lewis is lately married to Miss Lewis of the *bird.* The bridegroom was 18 and she 15. Young Mr. Monroe and a Miss Elisabeth Carr1 daughter of old Jemmy Carr have followed their example. Polly and My self have planted the cypress vine in boxes in the window as also date seeds and some other flowers. I hope you have not forgot the colection of garden seed you promised me for Bruni. I am under some obligation to her for several things which she has sent me and for which tho not yet come to hand I am not the less grateful. Flower seeds and fruit stones would no doubt be also very acceptable tho *grain de jardinage* was the expression she made use of. I will send you a letter to go with the seeds or be burnt if you cannot get them. I should be extremely obliged to you My Dearest Papa for a green silk calash lined with green also, as a hat is by no means proper for such a climate as ours. The little girl grows astonishingly and has been uncommonly healthy. Adieu My dear Papa. I have read gregory and am happy to tell you it was precisely the plan which we had followed with her for her birth by Mrs. Lewis's advice. We continue very great friends. She allways calls the child (who till you send her one will go by no other name) her grand daughter. Once more adieu my Dearest Papa your affectionate child,

M. Randolph[44]

[44] "To Thomas Jefferson from Martha Jefferson Randolph, 22 March 1791," *Founders Online,* National Archives, last modified June 13, 2018, http://founders.archives.gov/documents/Jefferson/01-19-02-0160.

My dear daughter

The badness of the roads retards the post, so that I have recieved no letter this week from Monticello. I shall hope soon to have one from yourself to know from that that you are perfectly reestablished, that the little Anne is becoming a big one, that you have received Dr. Gregory's book and are daily profiting from it.—This will hardly reach you in time to put you on the watch for the annular eclipse of the sun which is to happen on Sunday sennight to begin about sun-rise. It will be such a one as is rarely to be seen twice in one life. I have lately recieved a letter from Fulwar Skipwith who is consul for us in Martinique and Guadaloupe. He fixed himself first in the former, but has removed to the latter. Are any of your acquaintances in either of those islands? If they are, I wish you would write to them and recommend him to their acquaintance. He will be a sure medium thro which you may exchange *souvenirs* with your friends, of a more useful kind than those of the convent. He sent me half a dozen pots of very fine sweet-meats. Apples and cyder are the greatest presents which can be sent to those islands. I can make those presents for you whenever you chuse to write a letter to accompany them, only observing the season for apples. They had better deliver their letters for you to F. Skipwith. Things are going on well in France, the revolution being past all danger. The national assembly being to separate soon, that event will seal the whole with security. Their islands, but most particularly St. Domingue and Martinique are involved in a horrid civil war. Nothing can be more distressing than the situation of the inhabitants, as their slaves have been called into action, and are a terrible engine, absolutely ungovernable. It is worst in Martinique, which was the reason Mr. Skipwith left it. An army and fleet from France are expected every hour to quell the disorders.—I suppose you are busily engaged in your garden. I expect full details from you on that subject, as well as from Poll, that I may judge what sort of a gardener you make. Present me affectionately to all around you and be assured of the tender & unalterable love of Your's,

Th: Jefferson[45]

[45] "From Thomas Jefferson to Martha Jefferson Randolph, 24 March 1791," *Founders Online,* National Archives, last modified June 13, 2018, http://founders.archives.gov/documents/Jefferson/01-19-02-0165.

My Dear Daughter

Since I wrote last to you, which was on the 24th. of March, I have received yours of March 22. I am indeed sorry to hear of the situation of Walker Gilmer and shall hope the letters from Monticello will continue to inform me how he does. I know how much his parents will suffer, and how much he merited all their affection.—Mrs. Trist has been so kind as to have your calash made, but either by mistake of the maker, or of myself, it is not lined with green. I have therefore desired a green lining to be got, which you can put in yourself if you prefer it. Mrs. Trist has observed that there is a kind of veil lately introduced here, and much approved. It fastens over the brim of the hat and then draws round the neck as close or open as you please. I desire a couple to be made to go with the calash and other things.—Mr. Lewis not liking to write letters I do not hear from him: but I hope you are readily furnished with all the supplies and conveniences the estate affords. I shall not be able to see you till September, by which time the young-grandaughter will begin to look bold, and knowing. I inclose you a letter to a woman, who lives, I believe, on Buckisland. It is from her sister in Paris, which I would wish you to send express. I hope your garden is flourishing. Present me affectionately to Mr. Randolph & Polly. Your's sincerely my dear,

Th: Jefferson[46]

---

[46] "From Thomas Jefferson to Martha Jefferson Randolph, 17 April 1791," *Founders Online,* National Archives, last modified June 13, 2018, http://founders.archives.gov/documents/Jefferson/01-20-02-0052.

Monticello May 23, 1791

My Dear Papa

As you have been so long without hearing from any of us Mr. Randolph begged me to write a few lines to you that you might not be uneasy. He had began to do it himself but was prevented by a very bad cut in his thumb. It is almost 5 weeks since I have recieved a letter from you which I attribute to the irregularity of the post: that of Charlottesville they say is reestablished. Anthony has been to innoculate your trees. We had strawberries here the 2d of this month and cherries I think the 9th tho they had had both some time before that at Richmond. As I did not expect to have written this week it was so late before I began that I am obliged to be very concise for fear of missing the post which is expected in town early this morning and by which I am in hopes of recieving a letter from you. Adieu My Dear Papa. We have all been in perfect health here and are extremly obliged to you for the veils you sent us. I am with the tenderest love your affectionate child,

M. Randolph

The largest of the beans you sent me is come up and very flourishing but none of the others have as yet made their appearance.[47]

[47] "To Thomas Jefferson from Martha Jefferson Randolph, 23 May 1791," *Founders Online,* National Archives, last modified June 13, 2018, http://founders.archives.gov/documents/Jefferson/01-20-02-0177.

My dear Martha

I wrote to Maria yesterday, while sailing on Lake George, and the same kind of leisure is afforded me today to write to you. Lake George is without comparison the most beautiful water I ever saw: formed by a contour of mountains into a bason 35 miles long, and from 2 to 4 miles broad, finely interspersed with islands, its waters limpid as chrystal and the mountain sides covered with rich groves of Thuya, silver fir, white pine, Aspen and paper birch down to the water edge, here and there precipices of rock to checquer the scene and save it from monotony. An abundance of speckled trout, salmon trout, bass and other fish with which it is stored, have added to our other amusements the sport of taking them. Lake Champlain, tho much larger, is a far less pleasant water. It is muddy, turbulent, and yields little game. After penetrating into it about 25 miles we have been obliged by a head wind and high sea to return, having spent a day and a half in sailing on it. We shall take our rout again thro Lake George, pass thro Vermont down Connecticut river, and through Long island to New York and Philadelphia. Our journey hitherto has been prosperous and pleasant except as to the weather which has been as sultry hot through the whole as could be found in Carolina or Georgia. I suspect indeed that the heats of Northern climates may be more powerful than those of Southern ones in proportion as they are shorter. Perhaps vegetation requires this. There is as much fever and ague too and other bilious complaints on Lake Champlain as on the swamps of Carolina. Strawberries here are in the blossom, or just formed. With you I suppose the season is over. On the whole I find nothing any where else in point of climate which Virginia need envy to any part of the world. Here they are locked up in ice and snow for six months. Spring and autumn, which make a paradise of our country, are rigorous winter with them, and a Tropical summer breaks on them all at once. When we consider how much climate

75

contributes to the happiness of our condition, by the fine sensations it excites, and the productions it is the parent of, we have reason to value highly the accident of birth in such an one as that of Virginia.

From this distance I can have little domestic to write to you about. I must always repeat how much I love you. Kiss the little Anne for me. I hope she grows lustily, enjoys good health, and will make us all and long happy as the center of our common love. Adieu my dear. Your's affectionately,

Th: Jefferson[48]

[48] "V. Thomas Jefferson to Martha Jefferson Randolph, 31 May 1791," *Founders Online,* National Archives, last modified June 13, 2018, http://founders.archives.gov/documents/Jefferson/01-20-02-0173-0006.

My dear daughter

I wrote to each of you once during my journey, from which I returned four days ago, having enjoyed thro' the whole of it very perfect health. I am in hopes the relaxation it gave me from business has freed me from the almost constant headach with which I had been persecuted thro the whole winter and spring. Having been entirely clear of it while travelling proves it to have been occasioned by the drudgery of business. I found here on my return your letter of May 23. with the pleasing information that you were all in good health. I wish I could say when I shall be able to join you: but that will depend on the movements of the President who is not yet returned to this place.—In a letter written me by young Mr. Franklin, who is in London, is the following paragraph. 'I meet here with many who ask kindly after you, among these the D. of Dorset, who is very particular in his enquiries. He has mentioned to me that his niece had wrote once or twice to your daughter since her return to America; but not receiving an answer had supposed she meant to drop her acquaintance, which his neice much regretted. I ventured to assure him that that was not likely, and that possibly the letters might have miscarried.—You will take what notice of this you may think proper.'—Fulwar Skipwith is on his return to the United States.—Mrs. Trist and Mrs. Waters often ask after you.—Mr. Lewis being very averse to writing, I must trouble Mr. Randolph to enquire of him relative to my tobacco, and to inform me about it. I sold the whole of what was good here. 17. hogsheads only are yet come, and by a letter of May 29. from Mr. Hylton there were then but 2. hogsheads more arrived at the warehouse. I am uneasy at the delay, because it not only embarrasses me with guessing at excuses to the purchaser, but is likely to make me fail in my payment to Hanson, which ought to be made in Richmond on the 19th. of next month. I wish much to know when the rest may be expected.—In your last you observe you had not received a letter from me in five weeks. My letters to you have been of Jan. 20. Feb. 9. Mar. 2. 24. Apr. 17. May 8. which you will observe to be pretty regularly once in three weeks.—Matters in France are still going on safely. Mirabeau is dead; also the Duke de Richlieu; so that the Duke de Fronsac has now succeeded to the head of the family, tho' not to the title, these being all abolished. Present me affectionately to Mr. Randolph and Polly, and kiss the little one for me: Adieu my dear Your's affectionately,

Th: Jefferson[49]

---

[49] "From Thomas Jefferson to Martha Jefferson Randolph, 23 June 1791," *Founders Online,* National Archives, last modified June 13, 2018, http://founders.archives.gov/documents/Jefferson/01-20-02-0217.

Philadelphia July 10. 1791.

My dear Daughter

I have no letter from Monticello later than Maria's of May 29. which is now six weeks old. This is long, when but one week is necessary for the conveyance. I cannot ascribe all the delay to the Charlottesville post. However to put that out of the way I am negotiating with the postmaster the establishment of a public post from Richmond to Staunton. In this case all the private riders will be prohibited from continuance, let their contracts be what they will, and the whole being brought into one hand, the public will be better served. I propose that the post shall pass by Tuckahoe, Goochld. courthouse, Columbia and Charlottesville in order that as many may be served by it as possible. The price on each newspaper will be to be settled between the printers and their customers.—I have no information whether the things sent by Stratton have got safe to hand: tho' hope they have. I expect him here daily, and shall send by him some stores against my arrival at Monticello, the time of which however is not yet fixable. I rather expect it will be earlier than the last year, because my return here must be earlier. Tell Maria I shall expect to find her improved in all good things and particularly in her music, of which I hope you also are mindful. Kiss her for me and the little one, and present my best esteem to Mr. Randolph.—Your's, my dear, affectionately,

Th: Jefferson[50]

[50] "From Thomas Jefferson to Martha Jefferson Randolph, 10 July 1791," *Founders Online,* National Archives, last modified June 13, 2018, http://founders.archives.gov/documents/Jefferson/01-20-02-0268.

My dear daughter

Your last letter come to hand was of May 23. Consequently it is now two months old.

Petit arrived here three or four days ago, and accosted me with an assurance that he was come pour rester toujours avec moi. The principal small news he brings is that Panthemont is one of the convents to be kept up for education, that the old Abbess is living, but Madame de Taubenheim dead, that some of the nuns have chosen to rejoin the world, others to stay, that there are no English pensioners there now, Botidour remains there, &c. &c. &c. Mr. Short lives in the Hotel d'Orleans where I lived when you first went to Panthemont.

The President is indisposed with a complaint similar to that he had in New York the year before last. It is commonly called a blind bile, and is in fact a tumour which will not come to a head.—I do not yet know when I shall go to Virginia, and fear the visit will be short. It will probably be the beginning of September. I sent off yesterday by Capt. Stratton 4. boxes and 14. kegs with stores to be delivered to Mr. Brown to be forwarded to Monticello. But I beg you not to await my coming for the opening and using of them, as they are for the common use. Kiss Maria and the little Anne for me and accept cordial love from your's affectionately,

Th: J[51]

---

[51] "From Thomas Jefferson to Martha Jefferson Randolph, 24 July 1791," *Founders Online,* National Archives, last modified June 13, 2018, http://founders.archives.gov/documents/Jefferson/01-20-02-0319.

My dear daughter

Maria's letter of July 16. informs me you were all well then. However great my confidence is in the healthy air of Monticello, I am always happy to have my hopes confirmed by letter. The day of my departure is not yet fixed. I hope it will be earlier or later in the first week of September. I know not as yet how I am to get along, as one of my horses is in such a condition as to leave little hope of his life, and no possibility of his being in a condition to travel. I hope, before you recieve this, the articles sent by Capt Stratton will be come to hand.—The moment affording nothing new but what the gazettes will communicate, I have only to add my affections to Mr. Randolph & Maria, not forgetting the little one, and to yourself my dear Martha the warm love of Your's affectionately,

Th: Jefferson[52]

[52] "From Thomas Jefferson to Martha Jefferson Randolph, 14 August 1791," *Founders Online,* National Archives, last modified June 13, 2018, http://founders.archives.gov/documents/Jefferson/01-22-02-0041.

My: dear Martha

Maria and myself are waiting with impatience to hear that Mr. Randolph and yourself and dear little Anne are well. We now write alternately, once a week, so that the correspondence is become more equal. I now inclose to Mr. Randolph Freneau's paper instead of Bache's on account of the bulk of the latter which, being a daily paper, was too much for the post. And Freneau's two papers contain more good matter than Bache's six. He will see that the affairs of the French West Indies are in a desperate state. A second set of deputies has arrived here to ask succours. Abundance of women and children come here to avoid danger. The men are not permitted to come. I should not wonder to see some of your friends among them.—We expect hourly the arrival of Capt. Stratton, by whom the clothes for the house servants shall be sent. To forward them by any other vessel, is risking their miscarriage. Maria is fixed at Mrs. Pine's, and perfectly at home. She has made young friends enough to keep herself in a bustle with them, and she has been honored with the visits of Mrs. Adams, Mrs. Randolph, Mrs. Rittenhouse, Sarjeant, Waters, Davies &c., so that she is quite familiar with Philadelphia. Present my sincere attachment to Mr. Randolph and kiss Anne for us. Adieu my dear, dear daughter. Your's affectionately,

Th: Jefferson[53]

[53] "From Thomas Jefferson to Martha Jefferson Randolph, 13 November 1791," *Founders Online,* National Archives, last modified June 13, 2018, http://founders.archives.gov/documents/Jefferson/01-22-02-0270.

Philadelphia Dec. 4. 1791.

My Dear Daughter

We are well here, tho' still without news from Mr. Randolph or yourself, tho' we have been eight weeks from Monticello. Maria was to have written to you to-day, but she has been so closely engaged in pasting paper together in the form of a pocket book that she has not been able. She has been constantly getting colds since she came here. I have put on board Capt Stratton a box with the following articles for your three house-maids.

36. yds. callimanco

13 1/2 hds. calico of different patterns

25. yds. linen

9. yds. muslin

9. pr. cotton stockings thread.

I put into the same box for you la Cuisiniere Bourgeoise and the following books which Mr. Randolph wished to see. Ginanni del grano—Duhamel, maniere de conserver le grain, Duhamel de l'insecte de l'Angoumois.— Mr. Randolph sees by the papers sent him what is the price of wheat here. Perhaps he might think it worth while to send his Varina wheat here. He could always have the money in Richmond within a fortnight from the arrival of the wheat. I shall be very ready to have it received and disposed of for him on the best terms, if he chuses. So as to corn or any thing else. My affectionate love attends you all. Adieu my dear dear daughter,

Th: Jefferson[54]

---

[54] "From Thomas Jefferson to Martha Jefferson Randolph, 4 December 1791," *Founders Online,* National Archives, last modified June 13, 2018, http://founders.archives.gov/documents/Jefferson/01-22-02-0340.

My Dear Daughter

Your's of Nov. 29. and Mr. Randolph's of Nov. 28. came to hand five days ago. They brought us the first news we had received from Monticello since we left it. A day or two after, Mr. Millar of Charlottesville arrived here and gave us information of a little later date, and particularly of Colo. Lewis and Mrs. Gilmer's illness. His account of Mrs. Gilmer was alarming, and I am anxious to hear it's issue. Our feelings on little Anne's danger as well as her escape were greatly excited on all your accounts. These alarms and losses are the price parents pay for the pleasure they recieve from their children. I hope her future good health will spare you any more of them.—We are likely to get a post established through Columbia, Charlottesville, and Staunton, on a permanent footing, and consequently a more regular one. This I hope will remove all precariousness in the transportation of our letters. Tho I am afraid there is one kind of precariousness it will not remove; that in the writing of them, for you do not mention having written before the 29th. of Nov. tho' we had then left Monticello near seven weeks: I have written every week regularly. Present me affectionately to Mr. Randolph. Kiss dear Anne for me, and believe me to be your's with tender love.

Th: Jefferson[55]

---

[55] "From Thomas Jefferson to Martha Jefferson Randolph, 25 December 1791," *Founders Online,* National Archives, last modified June 13, 2018, http://founders.archives.gov/documents/Jefferson/01-22-02-0419.

My dear Martha

Having no particular subject for a letter, I find none more soothing to my mind than to indulge itself in expressions of the love I bear you, and the delight with which I recall the various scenes thro which we have passed together, in our wanderings over the world. These reveries alleviate the toils and inquietudes of my present situation, and leave me always impressed with the desire of being at home once more, and of exchanging labour, envy, and malice, for ease, domestic occupation, and domestic love and society, where I may once more be happy with you, with Mr. Randolph, and dear little Anne, with whom even Socrates might ride on a stick without being ridiculous. Indeed it is with difficulty that my resolution will bear me through what yet lies between the present day and that which, on mature consideration of all circumstances respecting myself and others, my mind has determined to be the proper one for relinquishing my office. Tho' not very distant, it is not near enough for my wishes. The ardor of these however would be abated if I thought that on coming home I should be left alone. On the contrary I hope that Mr. Randolph will find a convenience in making only leisurely preparations for a settlement, and that I shall be able to make you both happier than you have been at Monticello, and relieve you from *desagremens* to which I have been sensible you were exposed, without the power in myself to prevent it, but by my own presence. Remember me affectionately to Mr. Randolph and be assured of the tender love of Yours,

Th: Jefferson[56]

---

[56] "From Thomas Jefferson to Martha Jefferson Randolph, 15 January 1792," *Founders Online,* National Archives, last modified June 13, 2018, http://founders.archives.gov/documents/Jefferson/01-23-02-0043.

My dear Martha

I was prevented writing to you last week by a bad cold attended with fever: and this week I have nothing to say but that I find myself nearly well, and to repeat the assurances of my love to you. Maria is well, and has come to a resolution to write to you no more. Whether this arises most from resentment or laziness I do not know. Mr. Randolph's last letter received was of Dec. 29, yours of Nov. 29. In my last to him, knowing that Clarkson could not write, I asked the favor of him to communicate to me from time to time the progress of my affairs. I wish much to know whether my wheat is getting to market, and the debts for which it was destined paying off? negroes clothed &c. Adieu my dear your's affectionately,

Th: Jefferson[57]

[57] "From Thomas Jefferson to Martha Jefferson Randolph, 5 February 1792," *Founders Online,* National Archives, last modified June 13, 2018, http://founders.archives.gov/documents/Jefferson/01-23-02-0101.

My Dearest Father

Just arrived from a journey of 3 months on which I have not had it in my power to write to you. I am impatient to take the first opportunity of renewing a correspondance so very pleasing to me. I recieved your letters all together at Dick Randolph's and should have answered them imediately but Mr. Randolph's writing rendered it unecessary at that time. We have had a most disagreable journey travelling greatest part of the way thro a deep snow and dismal weather generally raining or hailing. I never saw the end of any thing with more pleasure in my life. The anxiety you express to be at home makes me infinitely happy. I acknowledge I was under some aprehension that you would be prevailed upon to stay longer than you intended and I feel more and more every day how necessary your company is to my happiness by the continual and ardent desire I have of seeing you. I suppose Mr. Randolph has told you that he is in possession of Edgehill. The old gentleman has at Last made him a deed for it. He has also bought those negroes who had families here. We are so lately arrived that I have not heard any news as yet. Mrs. Gilmer has been in a state of insanity from which I *believe* she is recovered tho I am by no means certain. I have weaned Little Anne who begins to walk. She becomes every day more mischievious and more entertaining. I think she is also handsomer than the was and looks much better tho not as fat. Adieu my Dearest Papa. Tell me if we shall have the pleasure of seeing you this spring and believe me with tender and unchangeable love your affectionate child,

M. Randolph

My best love to Dear Maria. Tell her I will certainly write to her next week.[58]

[58] "To Thomas Jefferson from Martha Jefferson Randolph, 20 February 1792," *Founders Online,* National Archives, last modified June 13, 2018, http://founders.archives.gov/documents/Jefferson/01-23-02-0126.

My Dear Martha

We are in daily expectation of hearing of your safe return to Monticello, and all in good health. The season is now coming on when I shall envy your occupations in the feilds and garden, while I am shut up drudging within four walls. Maria is well and lazy, therefore does not write. Your friends Mrs. Trist and Mrs. Waters are well also, and often enquire after you. We have nothing new or interesting from Europe for Mr. Randolph. He will perceive by the papers that the English are beaten off the ground by Tippoo Saib. The Leyden gazette assures that they were saved only by the unexpected arrival of the Mahrattas, who were suing to Tippoo Saib for peace for Ld. Cornwallis.—My best esteem to Mr. Randolph, & I am my dear Martha your's affectionately,

Th: Jefferson[59]

---

[59] "From Thomas Jefferson to Martha Jefferson Randolph, 26 February 1792," *Founders Online,* National Archives, last modified June 13, 2018, http://founders.archives.gov/documents/Jefferson/01-23-02-0149.

My dear Martha

Yours of Feb. 20. came to me with that welcome which every thing brings from you. It is a relief to be withdrawn from the torment of the scenes amidst which we are. Spectators of the heats and tumults of conflicting parties, we cannot help participating of their feelings. I should envy you the tranquil occupations of your situation were it not that I value your happiness more than my own. But I too shall have my turn. The ensuing year will be the longest of my life, and the last of such hateful labours. The next we will sow our cabbages together. Maria is well. Having changed my day of writing from Sunday to Thursday or Friday, she will oftener miss writing, as not being with me at the time.—I believe you knew Otchakity the Indian who lived with the Marquis Fayette. He came here lately with some deputies from his nation, and died here of a pleurisy. I was at his funeral yesterday. He was buried standing up according to their manner. I think it will still be a month before your neighbor Mrs. Monroe will leave us. She will probably do it with more pleasure than heretofore; as I think she begins to tire of the town and feel a relish for scenes of more tranquillity. Kiss dear Anne for her aunt, and twice for her grandpapa. Give my best affections to Mr. Randolph and accept yourself all my tenderness.

Th: Jefferson[60]

---

[60] "From Thomas Jefferson to Martha Jefferson Randolph, 22 March 1792," *Founders Online,* National Archives, last modified June 13, 2018, http://founders.archives.gov/documents/Jefferson/01-23-02-0272.

Philadelphia Apr. 6. 1792.

My dear Martha

Mr. Randolph's letter of the 18th. has been received since my last. The one it covered for Great Britain is sent by the packet now about to sail from New York. His commission to Doctor Barton shall be fulfilled to-day. Maria is with me keeping her Easter holidays. She is well. She allows herself to write but one letter a week, and having written to some acquaintance already she has nothing but her love for Monticello.-I suppose you are busy in your garden. Shackleford promised me *on his honor* to cover it well with manure. Has he done it? If not, tell him I have written to enquire.-Two or three straggling numbers of Fenno's gazette being found in my office, we presume they belong to Mr. Randolph's set, and therefore I send them. Present my best affections to him, and be assured of the cordial love of Your's,

Th: Jefferson[61]

[61] "From Thomas Jefferson to Martha Jefferson Randolph, 6 April 1792," *Founders Online,* National Archives, last modified June 13, 2018, http://founders.archives.gov/documents/Jefferson/01-23-02-0333.

My dear daughter

I received yesterday your's and Mr. Randolph's of the 9th. which shews that the post somehow or other slips a week. Congress have determined to rise on the 5th. of May. Colo. Monroe and Mrs. Monroe will set out on the 7th. and making a short stay at Fredericksburg pass on to Albemarle. I have reason to expect that my visit to Virginia this year, instead of September as heretofore, will be about the last of July, and be somewhat longer than usual, as it is hoped Congress will meet later.—Tell Mr. Randolph that Mr. Hylton informs me 43. hhds. of my tobacco, meaning of my mark, are arrived at the warehouse, and that he shall send them on by the first opportunity. As this cannot possibly be all mine, it must contain Mr. Randolph's, and therefore it is necessary he should enable Mr. Hylton to distinguish his, or it will all come round here. I am to have 5. dollars for mine, payable in September, from which will be deducted about half a dollar expences. Maria is well and joins me in affections to Mr. Randolph and yourself. Adieu my dear. Your's &c.

Th: Jefferson[62]

---

[62] "From Thomas Jefferson to Martha Jefferson Randolph, 27 April 1792," *Founders Online,* National Archives, last modified June 13, 2018, http://founders.archives.gov/documents/Jefferson/01-23-02-0418.

My Dearest Papa

Mr. Randolph recieved your letter respecting the bonds 2 days before he set off for Richmond and carried them down with him. He has by Mr. Colquehoun's not appearing been cast in his suit with Rogers and fined 77 pounds which added to the other expences attending a suit amounts to upwards of a hundred. It is particularly unlucky at this time as he has met with many misfortunes which will render the payment of it rather distressing. I am rejoiced from my heart to hear that you are coming in july instead of september. You will see that I am a much tter gardner than last year tho in truth old George is so slow that shall never shine in that way with out your assistance. Tom has been a man of honour with respect to the manure. We have had some very high winds here lately one of which blew down 5 large trees in and about the grove and did some other mischief. It was accompanied with very severe lightning. The noise of the wind kept us from hearing any thing of the thunder except when it was extreemly loud. We have discoverd a very beautiful tree near the lower round about a silver fir I believe. It differs from the common pine in having a smooth green bark and the bottom of the leave white and much finer than the other. Mr. Randolph is still in Richmond. We are all well and Doctor Gilmer is perfectly recovered. My little Anne tho not handsome on account of her being allmost entirely bald is a source of infinite happyness to her fond Parents. She begins to prattle and is remarkably lively. Tell My Dearest Maria that I will write to her next week. Her friend Nancy Randolph is coming up with Mr. Randolph and Judy has a fine son. Adieu my dearest Father believe me your ever affectionate child,

M. Randolph[63]

[63] "To Thomas Jefferson from Martha Jefferson Randolph, 7 May 1792," *Founders Online,* National Archives, last modified June 13, 2018, http://founders.archives.gov/documents/Jefferson/01-23-02-0442.

Philadelphia May 11. 1792.

My dear daughter

Excess of business prevented my writing to you the last week or even having time to inclose the papers to Mr. Randolph. Since my last I have received yours of Feb. 28. and Mr. Randolph's of Apr. 9. 16. and May 4. Congress rose three days ago. Colo. Monroe sets out three days hence, and by him I shall send your watch, and the 2d. part of Payne's Rights of man for Mr. Randolph. Also, for yourself, my own copy of Lavater's aphorisms, which I fancy are not to be got here, and which I think you will sicken of in a few pages. Mrs. Pine has determined to go to England, so that I shall be obliged to send Maria to Mrs. Brodeau's, a better school, but much more distant from me. It will in fact cut off the daily visits which she is able to make me from Mrs. Pine's. I do not know whether I have before mentioned to you that the President will make his visit to Mount Vernon this year about the last of July: consequently mine to Monticello will be earlier than usual. Present my esteem to all my neighbors. My best affections to Mr. Randolph and yourself, not forgetting little Anne, who I suppose will be able to take a part in conversation by the time we see her. Adieu my dear dear daughter. Your's &c.

Th: Jefferson[64]

---

[64] "From Thomas Jefferson to Martha Jefferson Randolph, 11 May 1792," *Founders Online,* National Archives, last modified June 13, 2018, http://founders.archives.gov/documents/Jefferson/01-23-02-0453.

My dear daughter

I was too much occupied to write by Friday's post and fear it will occasion your recieving my letter a week later. Yours of the 7th. Inst. has come duly to hand. Colo. and Mrs. Monroe will probably be with you by the time you recieve this. Mr. Madison left us last Wednesday. I have promised, during his stay in Orange, to inclose to him Fenno's paper for his perusal, to be forwarded on to Mr. Randolph, which will sometimes occasion his recieving it later than he would have done. We expect the President tomorrow on his return from Mount-Vernon. To the news in the public papers I may add the attempt to assassinate the K. of Sweden. He was dangerously wounded. French affairs are going on pretty well. Their assignats begin to gain. The election in N. York will be interesting to Colo. Monroe. Tell him it is generally thought that Mr. Jay has the most votes, but that one of the returns which contains 1000 in his favor is so deficient that it is imagined the judges of the election (who are all Clintonians) will not recieve them, and this is a greater number than it is thought he has to spare, consequently he will fail in his election. My tobacco arrived here yesterday. I have constantly forgotten to make enquiry about my bacon. If it is not come from Monticello, I would rather it should remain there till I go home, as it will suffice if it is here by the opening of the next Congress. My best esteem to Colo. and Mrs. Monroe, Mr. Randolph and your friends with you. To yourself my tenderest affections. Adieu my dear daughter. Your's &c.,

Th: Jefferson[65]

---

[65] "From Thomas Jefferson to Martha Jefferson Randolph, 27 May 1792," *Founders Online,* National Archives, last modified June 13, 2018, http://founders.archives.gov/documents/Jefferson/01-23-02-0499.

I intended writing to My Dearest Father by the last post but being prevented I have taken this opportunity rather than differ it an other week. Young Nicholas Lewis is just returned from Williamsburg with his Lady whom I have not been to see as yet but I certainly intend it shortly. Altho I have some reason to complain of the airs that family has given themselves of late with me they find it so difficult to divest themselves of the authority they once enjoyed here that they continue to this day to exert it over every part of the enclosure to my great vexation as I look upon that to be my domain and of course infringing upon my rights to take any thing out of it with out my leave. I have however overlooked their impertinence with regard to that as I am determined not to fall out with them if I can possibly avoid it tho I acknowledge it hurts my pride not a little to be treated with so much contemt by those of whom I am conscious of not diserving it having allways been particularly attentive to the whole family as far as I had it in my power. I rejoice to think that this is the last year I have to put up with it. Bergere has six fine little puppies, all of which I am in hopes of being able to raise. They have been peculiarly unlucky with those in the past I believe. They have had no less than thirteen this spring of which six are dead probably starved to death. Many of your sugar maples are alive and tolerably flourishing considering the drouth. Your acasias are not come up yet tho they were planted imediately. We are burnt up for want of rain. The drouth has continued for upwards of 5 weeks and there is no appearance of its discontinuing as yet. People are in great pain about their crops. Indeed they have a wretched prospect before them and many of them are suffering for bread even at this time. Joseph Monroe has been extreemly ill but he is perfectly recoverd now. It is generally supposed it was the gout. We are all in perfect health here my self particularly. I do not recolect ever to have been as fat as I am at present. Adieu my dearest father. Beleive me ever yours most affectionately,

M. Randolph[66]

---

[66] "To Thomas Jefferson from Martha Jefferson Randolph, 27 May 1792," *Founders Online,* National Archives, last modified June 13, 2018, http://founders.archives.gov/documents/Jefferson/01-23-02-0500.

Philadelphia June 8. 1792.

My dear daughter

The last news we have from Monticello is by your letter of May 7. I am in hopes tomorrow's post will bring us something, for some how or other your letters (if you write by post to Richmond) miss a post and are sometimes a week longer coming than they ought to be.—The news from the French West India islands is more and more discouraging. Swarms of the inhabitants are quitting them and coming here daily. I wonder that none of your acquaintances write to you. Perhaps they may be in Martinique where the disturbance is not yet considerable. Perhaps they may be gone to France.—Your friend Mrs. Waters is in a fair way of losing her husband, as he appears to be in a galloping consumption. The family are alarmed at his situation, tho he goes about his business still with activity. Maria's letter will inform you she is well. Present me affectionately to Mr. Randolph, kiss dear Anne for me, and be assured of my tender love. Your's &c.

Th: Jefferson[67]

[67] "From Thomas Jefferson to Martha Jefferson Randolph, 8 June 1792," *Founders Online,* National Archives, last modified June 13, 2018, http://founders.archives.gov/documents/Jefferson/01-24-02-0039.

Philadelphia June 22. 1792.

My dear Martha

Yours of May 27. came to hand on the very day of my last to you, but after it was gone off. That of June 11. was received yesterday. Both made us happy in informing us you were all well. The rebuke to Maria produced the inclosed letter. The time of my departure for Monticello is not yet known. I shall within a week from this time send off my stores as usual that they may arrive before me. So that should any waggons be going down from the neighborhood it would be well to desire them to call on Mr. Brown in order to take up the stores should they be arrived.—I suspect by the account you give me of your garden, that you mean a surprise, as good singers always preface their performance by complaints of cold, hoarseness &c.—Maria is still with me. I am endeavoring to find a good lady to put her with if possible. If not, I shall send her to Mrs. Brodeaux as the last shift. Old Mrs. Hopkinson is living in town but does not keep house.—I am in hopes you have visited young Mrs. Lewis, and borne with the old one so as to keep on visiting terms. Sacrifices and suppressions of feeling in this way cost much less pain than open separation. The former are soon over: the latter haunt the peace of every day of one's life, be that ever so long. Adieu my dear, with my best affections to Mr. Randolph. Anne enjoys them without valuing them.

Th: Jefferson[68]

[68] "From Thomas Jefferson to Martha Jefferson Randolph, 22 June 1792," *Founders Online,* National Archives, last modified June 13, 2018, http://founders.archives.gov/documents/Jefferson/01-24-02-0108.

Dear Papa

I have just recieved yours of June 22. The sudden departure of the post who entered Charlottesville the morning and left it before dinner prevented my writing Last week tho Mr. Randolph did and sent his letter after him as far as fluvana courthouse before they could overtake him. To his iregularity is owing that which you complain of in the receipt of my letters. I am very sorry you cannot fix the time of your departure. As it aproches my anxiety augments. All other thoughts give way to that of shortly seeing two people so infinitely dear to me. What I told you of my garden is really true. Indeed if you see it at a distance it looks very green but it does not bear close examination the weeds having taken possession of much the greater part of it. Old George is so slow that by the time he has got to the end of his labour he has it all to do over again. 2 of the acasia's are come up and are flourishing. I have visited the two Mrs. Lewis's. The young lady appears to be a good little woman tho most intolerable weak. However she will be a near neighbor and of course worth cultivating. Dear little Anna has been in very bad health her illness having been occasioned by worms. Dr. Gilmer advised the tincture of sacre the effects of which were allmost imediate. She still looks badly but I imagine that may be partly owing to her cutting teeth. I must now trouble you with some little commissions of mine. The glass of one of those handsome engravings I brought in with me has by some accident got broke and not being able to suply the place of it in Richmond I should be extremely obliged to you to bring me one according to the measure and also a small frame with a glass to it for a picture of the size of the enclosed oval paper. Adieu my dear papa. The heat is incredible here. The thermometer has been at 96 in Richmond and even at this place we have not been able to sleep comfortably with every door and window open. I dont recolect ever to have suffered as much from heat as we have done this summer. Adieu my Dearest Father. Believe me with tender affection yours

M. Randolph[69]

---

[69] "To Thomas Jefferson from Martha Jefferson Randolph, 2 July 1792," *Founders Online,* National Archives, last modified June 13, 2018, http://founders.archives.gov/documents/Jefferson/01-24-02-0151.

My dear Martha

I now inclose you Petit's statement of the stores sent round to Richmond to the care of Mr. Brown. They sailed from hence yesterday morning, and the winds have been and are so favorable that I dare say they will be in Chesapeak bay tomorrow, ready for the first Southernly breeze to carry them up the river. So that they will probably be at Richmond some days before you receive this. I wrote to Mr. Randolph last week desiring he would speak to Mr. Claxton to get the stores brought up immediately, which I hope he is doing, as I shall otherwise arrive before them. The President has fixed his departure on Thursday the 12th. inst. and I consequently fix mine to Saturday the 14th. According to the stages I have marked out, I shall be at Mr. Madison's on Saturday the 21st. and if on that day you can send a pair of the plough or waggon horses to John Jones's, 17. miles from Monticello and about 12. miles from Mr. Madison's, I can be at Monticello the next morning by 10. or 11. aclock. I do not know whether Jones's is a tavern, but he surely will give them cover the Saturday night, if they carry their own provision, and even a day or two longer, should any accident retard me in my departure or on the road. The road from Jones's to Monticello is so excessively hilly that it will injure my horses more than all the rest of the journey, as they will by that time be jaded with the heat. If I have rightly estimated the course of the post, you will recieve this on Saturday the 14th. the very day I leave Philadelphia. I shall write you again the day before I leave Philadelphia, which I presume you will receive on Saturday the 21st. in the morning of which day I expect to arrive at Mr. Madison's, unless any thing should arise to retard me, in which case that letter will probably give you notice of it. A Mr. Williams handed me yesterday a letter from Mr. Randolph. He was much gratified with the sight of my paintings. Mr. Randolph's desire shall be complied with. Petit's note will enable you to open any of the stores you may have occasion for, which I beg you not to hesitate to do, as they are intended more for you than myself. My best esteem to Mr. Randolph, and beleive me to be, my dear Martha, with the most tender affection Your's

Th: Jefferson[70]

[70] "From Thomas Jefferson to Martha Jefferson Randolph, 3 July 1792," *Founders Online,* National Archives, last modified June 13, 2018, http://founders.archives.gov/documents/Jefferson/01-24-02-0160.

Philadelphia July 13. 1792.

My dear Martha

Yours of the 2d came yesterday. I wrote to Mr. Randolph two days ago, but by a bungle of the servant it did not get to the post office in time, so I suppose that and this will get to hand together, and both probably only the evening before I shall reach Monticello. Still should my former one desiring horses, have missed, this will be in time for them to meet me on the road, and relieve mine in the last and worst part of it.

I set out this afternoon, and can pretty certainly be with you early on Sunday Sennight. My affections to Mr. Randolph. Adieu my dear.

Th: Jefferson[71]

---

[71] "From Thomas Jefferson to Martha Jefferson Randolph, 13 July 1792," *Founders Online,* National Archives, last modified June 13, 2018, http://founders.archives.gov/documents/Jefferson/01-24-02-0215.

Philadelphia Oct. 26. 1792.

My dear daughter

Having not received a letter by yesterday's post, and that of the former week from Mr. Randolph having announced dear Anne's indisposition, I am under much anxiety. In my last letter to Mr. Randolph I barely mentioned your being recovered, when somewhat younger than she is, by recurrence to a good breast of milk. Perhaps this might be worthy of proposing to the Doctor. In a case where weakness of the digesting organs enters into the causes of illness, a food of the most easy digestion might give time for getting the better of the other causes, whatever they may be. I think it should however be some other than your own, if a breast of milk is to be tried.—I hope you are perfectly well and the little one also, as well as Mr. Randolph to whom present my sincere regards. Adieu my dear your's affectionately

Th: Jefferson[72]

My dear Martha

The last post day for Monticello, which was the 9th. slipt by me without my recollecting it. However as you are perhaps in Cumberland, a letter of this day may get to you only three days the later. I have nothing indeed to tell you but that I love you dearly, and your dear connections, that I am well, as is Maria. I hope your little one has felt no inconvenience from the journey, that Anne is quite recovered, and Mr. Randolph's health good. Yours is so firm, that I am less apt to apprehend for you: Still, however, take care of your good health, and of your affection to me, which is the solace of my life. Remember me cordially to Mr. Randolph. Yours &c

Th. Jefferson[73]

---

[73] "From Thomas Jefferson to Martha Jefferson Randolph, 12 November 1792," *Founders Online,* National Archives, last modified June 13, 2018, http://founders.archives.gov/documents/Jefferson/01-24-02-0579.

I am afraid my dear Papa has by this time allmost dispaired of ever recieving another line from me. I have no excuse for having neglected writing entirerly, tho a very good one for not doing it often, my mind has been in such a continual state of anxiety on account of Anne as to render me unfit for any thing. The hopes I had concieved of her recovery are all blasted by a relapse and that too at the time she appeard out of all danger. Every moment of my life is embitered by the aprehensions of losing her. Indeed she has for many months been an untarissable source of pain to me and will I fear continue so for the weakness of her constitution is such that the smallest excess in her diet brings on her disorder. Your Little name sake is a remarckably fine boy. He bore the fatigue of the journey better than any of us. Adieu my dear Papa. You must excuse this scrawl. It is written by the bed side where my little angel lies with a high fever upon her and Mr. Randolph's absence at this time adds greatly to my distress. Once more adieu and believe me dearest father with unalterable love yours

M. Randolph

Give my love to dear Maria. Tell her I have recieved her letter and will answer it as soon as I have it in my power.[74]

---

[74] "To Thomas Jefferson from Martha Jefferson Randolph, 18 November 1792," *Founders Online,* National Archives, last modified June 13, 2018, http://founders.archives.gov/documents/Jefferson/01-24-02-0613.

My dear Martha

The last letter received from Mr. Randolph or yourself is of Oct. 7. which is near seven weeks ago. I ascribe this to your supposed absence from Monticello, but it makes me uneasy when I recollect the frail state of your two little ones. I hope some letter is on the way to me. I have no news for you except the marriage of your friend Lady Elizabeth Tufton, to some very rich person, but whose name could not be recollected by Mr. Hammond, my informer. Maria is well, but not yet become industrious in letter writing. Present my warmest esteem to Mr. Randolph. Adieu my dear your's affectionately & for ever

Th: J.[75]

[75] "From Thomas Jefferson to Martha Jefferson Randolph, 22 November 1792," *Founders Online,* National Archives, last modified June 13, 2018, http://founders.archives.gov/documents/Jefferson/01-24-02-0638.

Philadelphia Dec. 6. 92.

My dear Martha

I have this day received yours of the 18th. November and sincerely sympathize with you on the state of dear Anne, if that can be called sympathy which proceeds from affection at first hand, for my affections had fastened on her for her own sake and not merely for yours. Still however experience (and that in your own case) has taught me that an infant is never desperate, let me beseech you not to destroy the powers of her stomach with medecine. Nature alone can re-establish infant-organs; only taking care that her efforts be not thwarted by any imprudencies of diet. I rejoice in the health of your other hope. Maria is well. Remember me affectionately to Mr. Randolph and be assured of my unceasing love for you both. Adieu my very dear Martha

Th: Jefferson[76]

---

[76] "From Thomas Jefferson to Martha Jefferson Randolph, 6 December 1792," *Founders Online,* National Archives, last modified June 13, 2018, http://founders.archives.gov/documents/Jefferson/01-24-02-0692.

My dear Martha

By capt. Swaile, who sailed yesterday for Richmond I sent addressed to Mr. Randolph to the care of Mr. Brown a box containing the following articles for your three house maids.

2. peices of linen. 52. yards

9. pair cotton stockings (3 of them small)

13. yds. cotton in three patterns

36. yards Calimanco.

9. yards muslin.

Bob is to have a share of the linen. I had promised to send him a new suit of clothes. Instead of this I send a suit of superfine ratteen of my own, which I have scarcely ever worn. I forgot to get stockings for him: therefore must desire you to have him furnished with them from Colo. Bell's on my account.—In the same box you will find 4. pair tongs and shovels which I observed the house to be in want of. I hope our dear Anne is got well and that all of you continue so. Maria is well. She begun a letter to you Sunday was sennight: but it is not finished. My affections to Mr. Randolph and your friends. Adieu, my dear, yours with all love

Th: Jefferson[77]

---

[77] "From Thomas Jefferson to Martha Jefferson Randolph, 13 December 1792," *Founders Online,* National Archives, last modified June 13, 2018, http://founders.archives.gov/documents/Jefferson/01-24-02-0723.

My dear Martha

I received three days ago Mr. Randolph's letter of the 14th. from Richmond, and received it with great joy as it informed me of the reestablishment of dear Anne's health. I apprehend from an expression in his letter that some of mine may have miscarried. I have never failed to write every Thursday or Friday. Percieving by the Richmond paper that the Western post now leaves that place on Monday, I change my day of writing also to Sunday or Monday.—One of the Indian chiefs now here, whom you may remember to have seen at Monticello a day or two before Tarlton drove us of, remembers you and enquired after you. He is of the Pioria nation. Perhaps you may recollect that he gave our name to an infant son he then had with him and who, he now tells me, is a fine lad.— Blanchard is arrived here and is to ascend in his balloon within a few days. The affairs of France are going on well.—Tell Mr. Randolph that I write him a letter by this post in answer to the application to rent Elkhill; but under the possibility that the sale of it may be completed, I inclose his letter to Mr. Hylton with a desire that he will return it to me if the place is sold, otherwise to forward it to Mr. Randolph. My best esteem to him and our friends with you. Adieu, my dear, your's affectionately

Th: Jefferson[78]

[78] "From Thomas Jefferson to Martha Jefferson Randolph, 31 December 1792," *Founders Online,* National Archives, last modified June 13, 2018, http://founders.archives.gov/documents/Jefferson/01-24-02-0782.

My Dear Martha

Mr. Randolph's letter of Dec. 20. from Richmond is the only one come to hand from him or you since your's from Bizarre of two months ago. Tho' his letter informed me of the re-establishment of Anne, yet I wish to learn that time confirms our hopes. We were entertained here lately with the ascent of Mr. Blanchard in a baloon. The security of the thing appeared so great that every body is wishing for a baloon to travel in. I wish for one sincerely, as instead of 10. days, I should be within 5 hours of home. Maria will probably give you the baloon details, as she writes to-day.— Have you recieved the package with the servants clothes? My best attachments to Mr. Randolph. Adieu my dear Your's affectionately

Th: Jefferson[79]

---

[79] "From Thomas Jefferson to Martha Jefferson Randolph, 14 January 1793," *Founders Online,* National Archives, last modified June 13, 2018, http://founders.archives.gov/documents/Jefferson/01-25-02-0056.

With infinite pleasure I date once more from Monticello tho for the third time since my return but from the negligence of the servant that carried the letters once and the great hurry of the post another time they never got farther than Charlottesville. Our dearest Anne has had an attack of a different nature from her former ones which the doctor imagines to proceed from her fatening too quickly. She is far from being well yet, tho considerably better. She is at present busily employed *yiting* to you a thing she has never missed doing whenever her health has permitted her. Her memory is uncommonly good for a child of her age. She relates many circumstances that happened during her travels with great exactitude but in such broken language and with so many gestures as renders it highly diverting to hear her. Her spirits have as yet been proof against ill health so far as to recover them with the least inter mission of it tho I much fear that will not long be the case if she does not mend speedily. The little boy continues well and is little inferior to his sister in point of size. He also begins to take a great deal of notice and bids fair to be as lively. I am afraid you will be quite tired of hearing so much about them but a fond Mother never knows where to stop when her children is the subject. Mr. Randolph did not recieve the letter in which you mentioned the books and stalactite till after he had left Richmond with 4 or 5 other Letters of yours which had been detained by some accident. Peter desires to be remembered to you and wishes to know if you have recieved one he wrote you from Richmond. Adieu dearest Papa. My Love to dear Maria. I will write to her by the next post. Believe me to with tenderest affection yours

M. Randolph[80]

[80] "To Thomas Jefferson from Martha Jefferson Randolph, 16 January 1793," *Founders Online,* National Archives, last modified June 13, 2018, http://founders.archives.gov/documents/Jefferson/01-25-02-0074.

My Dear Martha

I received two days ago your's of the 16th. You were never more mistaken than in supposing you were too long on the prattle &c. of little Anne. I read it with quite as much pleasure as you write it. I sincerely wish I could hear of her perfect reestablishment.—I have for some time past been under an agitation of mind which I scarcely ever experienced before, produced by a check on my purpose of returning home at the close of this session of Congress. My operations at Monticello had been all made to bear upon that point of time, my mind was fixed on it with a fondness which was extreme, the purpose firmly declared to the President, when I became assailed from all quarters with a variety of objections. Among these it was urged that my retiring just when I had been attacked in the public papers, would injure me in the eyes of the public, who would suppose I either withdrew from investigation, or because I had not tone of mind sufficient to meet slander. The only reward I ever wished on my retirement was to carry with me nothing like a disapprobation of the public. These representations have, for some weeks passed, shaken a determination which I had thought the whole world could not have shaken. I have not yet finally made up my mind on the subject, nor changed my declaration to the President. But having perfect reliance in the disinterested friendship of some of those who have counselled and urged it strongly, believing that they can see and judge better a question between the public and myself than I can, I feel a possibility that I may be detained here into the summer. A few days will decide. In the mean time I have permitted my house to be rented after the middle of March, have sold such of my furniture as would not suit Monticello, and am packing up the rest and storing it ready to be shipped off to Richmond as soon as the season of good sea-weather comes on. A circumstance which weighs on me next to the weightiest is the trouble which I foresee I shall be constrained to ask Mr. Randolph to

116

undertake. Having taken from other pursuits a number of hands to execute several purposes which I had in view for this year, I can not abandon those purposes and lose their labour altogether. I must therefore select the most important and least troublesome of them, the execution of my canal, and (without embarrassing him with any details which Clarkson and George are equal to) get him to tell them always what is to be done and how, and to attend to the levelling the bottom. But on this I shall write him particularly if I defer my departure.—I have not received the letter which Mr. Carr wrote to me from Richmond nor any other from him since I left Monticello. My best affections to him, Mr. Randolph & your fireside and am with sincere love my dear Martha yours

Th: J.[81]

[81] "From Thomas Jefferson to Martha Jefferson Randolph, 26 January 1793," *Founders Online,* National Archives, last modified June 13, 2018, http://founders.archives.gov/documents/Jefferson/01-25-02-0103.

Phila Feb. 11. 1793.

My Dear Martha

The hour of post is come and a throng of business allows me only to inform you we are well, and to acknolege the receipt of Mr. Randolph's letter of Jan. 24. With hopes that you are all so accept assurances of constant love to you all from your's my dear most affectionately

Th: J.[82]

[82] "From Thomas Jefferson to Martha Jefferson Randolph, 11 February 1793," *Founders Online,* National Archives, last modified June 13, 2018, http://founders.archives.gov/documents/Jefferson/01-25-02-0160.

Philadelphia Feb. 24. 1793.

My dear dear daughter

We have no letter from Monticello since Mr. Randolph's of Jan. 30. to Maria. However we hope you are all well and that there are letters on the road which will tell us so. Maria writes to-day. Congress will rise on Saturday next, a term which is joyous to all as it affords some relaxation of business to all. We have had the mildest winter ever known, having had only two snows to cover the ground, and these remained but a short time. Heavy rains now falling will render the roads next to impassable for the members returning home. Colo. Monroe will stay some days after the rising of Congress.—Bob was here lately, and as he proposed to return to Richmond and thence to Monticello I charged him with enquiring for the box with the servants clothes, should Mr. Randolph not yet have heard of it. It went from hence the 12th. of December by the Schooner Mary, Capt. Swaile, bound for Norfolk and Richmd. The capt. undertook to deliver it to Mr. Brown in Richmond. From these circumstances it may certainly be found. Perhaps however an enquiry at Norfolk may be necessary. Present me affectionately to Mr. Randolph. Kiss dear Anne and ask her if she remembers me and will write to me. Health to the little one and happiness to you all. Your's affectionately my dear

Th: Jefferson[83]

---

[83] "From Thomas Jefferson to Martha Jefferson Randolph, 24 February 1793," *Founders Online,* National Archives, last modified June 13, 2018, http://founders.archives.gov/documents/Jefferson/01-25-02-0233.

Dear Papa

I have just this moment recieved yours of Jan. 26, which by the negligence of the post has remained a fortnight longer than it ought to have done upon the road. We had already Learnt your resolution of continuing in Philadelphia by a Letter of a Later date to Mr. Randolph. I concieve your anxiety by what I feel my self. It was a cruel disapointment to me who had set my heart upon the pleasure of seeing you in march never to separate again farther than Edgehill. Having never in my life been more intent upon any thing I never bore a disappointment with so little patience. My Little cherubs have both been very sick Lately. The Little boy has recoverd but My dear Anna continues extremely unwell. Poor Jenny Cary has Lost her husband and her sister Lucy is married to a Mr. Teril with whom she goes to Kentucke this spring so that Aunt Carr will have only one of her children with her it being the intention of Sam to settle imediately upon his own Land in this neighbourhood. It is so Late that I shall not have time to write to dear Maria this evening indeed I am affraid she thinks I never intend it again and that that is the reason she has left off writing to me However I hope to redeem my credit by the next post. In the mean time present my tenderest affections to her and be assured dear and much loved Father that no one breathing possesses them more entirely than your self. Yours

M. Randolph

I have unintentionally hurt Petit by neglecting to mention him in my letters therefore I should be much obliged to you to say *bien des choses* to him or any other message you think proper. I am affraid you will scarcely be able to read my Letter but it is one o'clock and the post goes of by day break. Once more adieu dear Father.[84]

[84] "To Thomas Jefferson from Martha Jefferson Randolph, 27 February 1793," *Founders Online,* National Archives, last modified June 13, 2018, http://founders.archives.gov/documents/Jefferson/01-25-02-0261.

My dear daughter

Your letters of the 20th. and 27th. Feb. as well as Mr. Randolph's of the same dates, came to hand only yesterday. By this I percieve that your post must be under bad regulation indeed. I am sorry to learn that your garden is dismantled, and yourself thereby discoraged from attention to it. I beg that Mr. Randolph will employ the whole force, he has been so kind as to direct, in repairing the inclosure in preference to every other work I had proposed. Nothing can be placed in competition with the loss of the produce of the garden during the season, either for health or comfort, and my own are less dear and desireable to me than the health and comfort of yourself, Mr. Randolph and the little ones. I had hoped that from the same resources your supplies of wood in the winter would not have failed. I again repeat it that I wish every other object to be considered as secondary in my mind to your accomodation and insist that Mr. Randolph make the freest use of the people under his direction for his and your convenience in the first place. When I shall see you I cannot say: but my heart and thoughts are all with you till I do. I have given up my house here, and taken a small one in the country on the banks of the Schuylkill to serve me while I stay. We are packing all our superfluous furniture and shall be sending it by water to Richmond when the season becomes favorable. My books too, except a very few, will be packed and go with the other things, so that I shall put it out of my own power to return to the city again to keep house, and it would be impossible to carry on business in the winter at a country residence. Tho' this points out an ultimate term of stay here, yet my mind is looking to a much shorter one if the circumstances will permit it which broke in on my first resolution. Indeed I have it much at heart to be at home in time to run up the part of the house the latter part of the summer and fall which I had proposed to do in the spring. Maria is well. Whether she writes or no to-day I know not. My best affections to

Mr. Randolph; cherish your little ones for me, for I feel the same love for them as I did for yourself when of their age, and continue to me your own love which I feel to be the best solace remaining to me in this world. Adieu my dear your's affectionately

Th: Jefferson[85]

[85] "From Thomas Jefferson to Martha Jefferson Randolph, 10 March 1793," *Founders Online,* National Archives, last modified June 13, 2018, http://founders.archives.gov/documents/Jefferson/01-25-02-0314.

My dear daughter

I have nothing interesting to tell you from hence but that we are well, and how much we love you. From Monticello you have every thing to l write about which I have any care. How do my young chesnut trees? How comes on your garden? How fare the fruit blossoms &c. I sent to Mr. Randolph, I think, some seed of the Bent-grass which is much extolled. I now inclose you some seed which Mr. Hawkins gave me, the name of which I have forgotten: but I dare say it is worth attention. I therefore turn it over to you, as I should hope not to reap what would be planted here. Within about a week I remove into the country. Tell Mr. Randolph that I send Fenno's papers thro' Mr. Madison, who left this place with Colo. and Mrs. Monroe on the 20th. Give my best attachments to Mr. Randolph and kiss the little ones for me. Your's affectionately my dear

Th: Jefferson[86]

---

[86] "From Thomas Jefferson to Martha Jefferson Randolph, 24 March 1793," *Founders Online,* National Archives, last modified June 13, 2018, http://founders.archives.gov/documents/Jefferson/01-25-02-0410.

Philadelphia Apr. 8. 1793.

My dear Martha

Since my letter of the last week, Maria has received one from Mr. Randolph which lets us know you were all well. I wish I could say the same. Maria has for these three or four weeks been indisposed with little fevers, nausea, want of appetite, and is become weak. The Doctor thinks it proceeds from a weakness of the stomach, and that it will soon be removed.—I learn from the head of Elk that a person of the name of Boulding set out from thence some days ago, to view my lands with an intention to become a tenant. He carried a letter from Mr. Hollingsworth, whom I had desired to procure tenants for me; not addressed I beleive to any particular person. I am in hopes he will apply to Mr. Randolph. The lands I should first lease would be the upper tract joining Key: but if enough of them would join to take the whole lands on that side of the river, they might divide them as they pleased.—I have never heard yet whether you got the servants' clothes which were sent by water. I have got all my superfluous furniture packed and on board a vessel bound to Richmond, to which place she will clear out to-day. I have written to Mr. Brown to hire a Warehouse or rather Ware-room for it, there being 1300. cubical feet of it, which would fill a moderate room. Some packages containing looking glass will have to remain there till next winter I presume, as they can only be trusted by water. Indeed I do not know how the rest will be got up. However, on this subject I will write to Mr. Randolph the next week.—War is certainly declared between France, England and Holland. This we learn by a packet the dispatches of which came to hand yesterday. J. Eppes sets out for Virginia to-day, to go and finish his course of study at Wm. and Mary. Tell Mr. Carr his letter is just now received, and shall be answered the next week, as I am now in the throng of my removal into the country. Remember me affectionately to him, to Mr. Randolph and kiss the little ones for me. Adieu my dear. Your's most affectionately

Th: J.[87]

---

[87] "From Thomas Jefferson to Martha Jefferson Randolph, 8 April 1793," *Founders Online,* National Archives, last modified June 13, 2018, http://founders.archives.gov/documents/Jefferson/01-25-02-0479.

My Dear Martha

I am now very long without a letter from Monticello, which is always a circumstance of anxiety to me. I wish I could say that Maria was quite well. I think her better for this week past, having for that time been free from the little fevers which had harrassed her nightly.—A paper which I some time ago saw in the Richmond gazette under the signature of R.R. proved to me the existence of a rumor, which I had otherwise heard of with less certainty. It has given me great uneasiness because I know it must have made so many others unhappy, and among these Mr. Randolph and yourself. Whatever the case may be, the world is become too rational to extend to one person the acts of another. Every one at present stands on the merit or demerit of their own conduct. I am in hopes therefore that neither of you feel any uneasiness but for the pitiable victim, whether it be of error or of slander. In either case I see guilt but in one person, and not in her. For her it is the moment of trying the affection of her friends, when their commiseration and comfort become balm to her wounds. I hope you will deal them out to her in full measure, regardless of what the trifling or malignant may think or say. Never throw off the best affections of nature in the moment when they become most precious to their object; nor fear to extend your hand to save another, lest you should sink yourself. You are on firm ground: your kindnesses will help her and count in your own favor also. I shall be made very happy if you are the instruments not only of supporting the spirits of your afflicted friend under the weight bearing on them, but of preserving her in the peace and love of her friends. I hope you have already taken this resolution if it were necessary; and I have no doubt you have: yet I wished it too much to omit mentioning it to you. I am with sincere love to Mr. Randolph & yourself, my dear Martha your's affectionately

Th: Jefferson[88]

---

[88] "From Thomas Jefferson to Martha Jefferson Randolph, 28 April 1793," *Founders Online,* National Archives, last modified June 13, 2018, http://founders.archives.gov/documents/Jefferson/01-25-02-0566.

Philadelphia May. 12. 1793.

My Dear Martha

I have at length found time to copy Petit's list of the packages sent to Richmond. Tho' I have not heard of their arrival there, I take for granted they must be arrived. I inclose you the list wherein I have marked with an * the boxes which must remain at Richmond till they can be carried up by water, as to put them into a waggon would be a certain sacrifice of them. They are the Nos. 2. 5. 10. 18. 19. 22. 23. 25. 26. 27. 28. Such of the others as contain any thing that you think would be convenient immediately, you may perhaps find means of having brought up. As to the rest, they may lie till I can have waggons of my own or find some other oeconomical means of getting them up. In any way it will be expensive, many of the boxes being enormously large.—I got a person to write to Scotland for a mason and house-joiner for me. I learn that they were engaged, and only waited for a ship. They will be delivered at Richmond to the address of Mr. Brown. A person who is come here, and knows them personally, says they are fine characters, will be very useful to have on a farm; it is material therefore that they do not remain 24. hours in Richmond to be spoiled. I shall write to Mr. Brown to send them off instantly and shall be obliged to Mr. Randolph to have an eye to the same object. How to employ them will be the subject of consideration. It will be puzzling till my return. It is one of the great inconveniences I experience by having been persuaded by my friends to defer carrying into execution my determination to retire. However when I see you, it will be never to part again. In the mean time my affairs must be a burthen to Mr. Randolph.—You have never informed me whether the box containing the servant's clothes, which were sent in December last, have been received. I am anxious to hear, because if it has not, I will prosecute the captain.— Maria's brain is hard at work to squeeze out a letter for Mr. Randolph. She has been scribbling and rubbing out these three hours, and this moment

129

exclaimed 'I do not think I shall get a letter made out to-day.'—We shall see how her labours will end. She wonders you do not write to her. So do I. Present me most affectionately to Mr. Randolph and be assured of my unceasing love to yourself. Kiss the dear little ones for me. Yours &c.

Th: Jefferson[89]

[89] "From Thomas Jefferson to Martha Jefferson Randolph, 12 May 1793," *Founders Online,* National Archives, last modified June 13, 2018, http://founders.archives.gov/documents/Jefferson/01-26-02-0014.

Dear Papa

I recieved your kind letter of April the 28 a week ago and should have answered it imediately but that the house was full of company at the time. The subject of it has been one of infinite anxiety both to Mr. Randolph and my self for many months and tho I am too sensible of the iliberality of extending to one person the infamy of an other, to fear one moment that it can reflect any real disgrace upon me in the eyes of people of sense yet the generality of mankind are weak enough to think otherwise and it is painful to an excess to be obliged to blush for so near a connection. I know it by fatal experience. As for the poor deluded victim I believe all feel much more for her than she does for her self. The villain having been no less successfull in corrupting her mind than he has in destroying her reputation. Amidst the distress of her family she alone is tranquil and seems proof against every other misfortune on earth but that of a separation from her vile seducer. They have been *tried* and acquited tho I am sorry to say his Lawers gained more honour by it than they did as but a small part of the world and those the most inconsiderable people in it were influenced in there opinion by the dicision of the court. In following the dictates of my own heart I was so happy as to stumble upon the very conduct you advised me to, before I knew your opinion. I have continued to behave with affection to her which her errors have not been able to eradicate from my heart and could I suppose her penitent, I would redouble my attentions to her though1 I am one of the few who have allways *doubted* the truth of the report. As the opinion I had of R. R. was most exalted would to heaven my hopes were equal to my fears but the latter often to often2 preside. The divisions of the family encrease daily. There is no knowing where they will end. The old gentleman has plunged into the thickest of them governed by the most childish passions he lends the little weight his imprudence has left him to widen the breaches it should be his duty to close. Mr. R—s conduct has been such as to conciliate the affections of the whole family. He is the Link by which so many discordant parts join. Having made up his difference with David Randolph there is not one individual but what Looks up to him as one, and the only one who has been uniform in his affection to them. My Little cherubs are both in perfect health. Anna was very much delighted with the *yather* and *fasty old bosselor* enclosed in it. She talks incessantly of you and Aunt Polly. Your chess nuts are all alive but *one* and the *acasia's* all dead but one. But that is very much grown and flourishing. Bergere has aded one to the number of genuine shepherds. The mungrels encrease upon us daily. My garden is in good order and would really cut a figure but for the worms and3 catipillars which abound so every where this year that they destroy the seed before it comes up and even the Leaves of the trees. Adieu my dear Papa. We are all impatient to see you. My love to Dear Maria and believe me ever yours,

m. randolph[90]

[90] "To Thomas Jefferson from Martha Jefferson Randolph, 16 May 1793," *Founders Online,* National Archives, last modified June 13, 2018, http://founders.archives.gov/documents/Jefferson/01-26-02-0042.

My dear Martha

Your and Mr. Randolph's welcome favors of the 16th. came to hand yesterday, by which I perceive that your post-day for writing is the Thursday. Maria is here and, tho not in flourishing health, is well. I will endeavour to prevail on her to write, and perhaps may succeed, as the day is too wet to admit her saunters on the banks of the Schuylkill, where she passes every Sunday with me. We are in sight both of Bartram's and Gray's gardens, but have the river between them and us.—We have two blind stories here. The one that Dumourier is gone over to the Austrians. The authority for this is an English paper. No confidence in DuMourier's virtue opposes it, for he has none: but the high reputation he has acquired is a pledge to the world, which we do not see that there were any motives on this occasion to induce him to forfeit. The other story is that he has cut off 10,000 Prussians, and among them the K. of Prussia and D. of Brunswick. The latter we know is out of command, and the former not in DuMourier's way. Therefore we concluded the story fabricated merely to set off against the other. It has now come thro' another channel and in a more possible form to wit that Custine has cut off 10,000 Prussians without naming the King or Duke. Still we give little ear to it.—You had at your Convent so many -courts (as terminations of names) that I wish the following paragraph of a newspaper may involve none of them. 'A few days ago several rich and respectable inhabitants were butchered at Guadaloupe. The following are the names of the unfortunate victims. Madame Vermont &c Madame Meyercourt. Monsr. Gondrecourt, three daughters just arrived from France from 11. to 18. years of age. Messrs. Vaudrecourt &c.' Maria thinks the Gondrecourts were at the convent.— The French minister Genet told me yesterday that matters appeared now to be tolerably well settled in St. Domingo. That the Patriotic party had taken possession of 600 aristocrats and monocrats, had sent 200 of them to

France, and were sending 400. here: and that a coalition had taken place among the other inhabitants. I wish we could distribute our 400 among the Indians, who would teach them lessons of liberty and equality. Give my best affections to Mr. Randolph and kiss the dear little ones for me. Adieu my very dear Martha. Your's constantly & affectionately

Th: Jefferson[91]

---

[91] "From Thomas Jefferson to Martha Jefferson Randolph, 26 May 1793," *Founders Online,* National Archives, last modified June 13, 2018, http://founders.archives.gov/documents/Jefferson/01-26-02-0115.

Philadelphia June 10. 93.

My dear Martha

I wrote you last on the 26th. of the last month. On the 3d. of the present I received Mr. Randolph's favor of May 22. I sincerely congratulate you on the arrival of the Mocking bird. Learn all the children to venerate it as a superior being in the form of a bird, or as a being which will haunt them if any harm is done to itself or it's eggs. I shall hope that the multiplication of the cedar in the neighborhood, and of trees and shrubs round the house, will attract more of them: for they like to be in the neighborhood of our habitations, if they furnish cover. I learn from Mr. Brown that all my furniture is safely arrived and stored at Rocket's. Maria is here, but too lazy to write. She says in excuse that you do not write to her.—Mrs. Shippen lost her little son Bannister the last week. He died of a dysentery. Our letters from Mr. Bev. Randolph and the other commissioners are that they were safely arrived at Niagara; and that their treaty was likely to be delayed a month longer than was expected. Consequently their return will be later. My sincere affections to Mr. Randolph and kiss dear Anne for me. Yours with constant love

Th: Jefferson[92]

---

[92] "From Thomas Jefferson to Martha Jefferson Randolph, 10 June 1793," *Founders Online,* National Archives, last modified June 13, 2018, http://founders.archives.gov/documents/Jefferson/01-26-02-0226.

Dear Papa

We recieved your 3 Last letters yesterday which by the carelessness of the post master in Richmond have been detained many weeks, indeed their negligence is intolerable, we have just heard of some of Mr. Randolphs Letters to you that have gone on to Lexington in kentucke. Those that we do get, come so irregularly without any regard to their dates that it is impossible to follow your directions with any degree of punctuality. Mr. Randolph thinks it would be most adviseable to have all your furniture brought by water as it is not only much more oeconomical but also safer. I have a terible account to give you of your cyder. Of 140 bottles that were put away you will hardly find 12. It flew in such a manner as to render it dangerous going near them. Those that were carelessly corked forced their corks the rest burst the bottles amongst which the havoc is incredible. The servants cloaths are not arrived nor have we been able to hear any thing about them. I am going on with such spirit in the garden that I think I shall conquer my *oponents* the *insects* yet, tho Hither to they have been as indifadigable in cutting up as I have been in planting. I have added to your accasia which is at Least 2 feet high 2 lemmon trees and have the promiss of an egg plant from Mr. Derieux. My dear little Anna daily more and more entertaining she is very observing and very talkative of course charming in the eyes of a mother. The dear Little boy tho not in perfect health is very well for one that is cutting teeth. *You* will easily concieve how great the satisfaction is I derive from the company of my sweet Little babes tho none but those who have experienced it can. I have allways forgot to mention Petit in any of my Letters. My negligence hurt his feelings I know, as it is not my design to do so you would oblige me infinitely by delivering some message to him *de ma part.* Adieu my dear Papa. Believe me with tender affection yours

M Randolph[93]

[93] "To Thomas Jefferson from Martha Jefferson Randolph, 26 June 1793," *Founders Online,* National Archives, last modified June 13, 2018, http://founders.archives.gov/documents/Jefferson/01-26-02-0344.

My Dear Daughter

My head has been so full of farming since I have found it necessary to prepare a plan for my manager, that I could not resist the addressing my last weekly letters to Mr. Randolph and boring him with my plans.—Maria writes to you to-day. She is getting into tolerable health, tho' not good. She passes two or three days in the week with me, under the trees, for I never go into the house but at the hour of bed. I never before knew the full value of trees. My house is entirely embosomed in high plane trees, with good grass below, and under them I breakfast, dine, write, read and receive my company. What would I not give that the trees planted nearest round the house at Monticello were full grown.—Can you make a provision of endive plants for the winter? Of celery I take for granted it may be done. But endive in great abundance would be a most valuable addition. I shall be in time for preparing covered places to transplant it to. Present me affectionately to Mr. Randolph and to the friends you have with you, and kiss the dear children for me. Adieu my dear. Yours with unceasing affection

Th: Jefferson[94]

---

[94] "From Thomas Jefferson to Martha Jefferson Randolph, 7 July 1793," *Founders Online,* National Archives, last modified June 13, 2018, http://founders.archives.gov/documents/Jefferson/01-26-02-0394.

Philadelphia July 21. 1793.

Th:J. to his dear daughter

We had peaches and Indian corn the 12th. instant. When do they begin with you this year?—Can you lay up a good stock of seed-peas for the ensuing summer? We will try this winter to cover our garden with a heavy coat of manure. When earth is rich it bids defiance to droughts, yeilds in abundance and of the best quality. I suspect that the insects which have harassed you have been encouraged by the feebleness of your plants, and that has been produced by the lean state of the soil.—We will attack them another year with joint efforts.—We learn that France has sent commissioners to England to treat of peace, and imagine it cannot be unacceptable to the latter, in the present state of general bankruptcy and demolition of their manufactures. Upon the whole the affairs of France, notwithstanding their difficulties external and internal, appear solid and safe. Present me to all my neighbors; kiss the little ones for me, and my warmest affections to yourself and Mr. Randolph.[95]

---

[95] "From Thomas Jefferson to Martha Jefferson Randolph, 21 July 1793," *Founders Online,* National Archives, last modified June 13, 2018, http://founders.archives.gov/documents/Jefferson/01-26-02-0481.

My dear Martha

I inclose you two of Petit's receipts. The orthography will amuse you, while the matter of them may be useful. The last of the two is really valuable, as the beans preserved in that manner, are as firm, fresh, and green, as when gathered.—Mr. D. Randolph is at Philadelphia, and well. He delivered me your watch, which I will have ready to send by him. He proposes to set out for Monticello in 8. or 10. days. Present my best respects to Mrs. Randolph and my regrets at my absence during the favor of her visit. I hope to be more fortunate another time.—We have had a remarkeable death here which I will mention for example sake. Mrs. Lear, wife of the gentleman who is secretary to the President, by eating green plumbs and apples brought on a mortification of the bowels which carried her off in six days. She was 23. years old, and of as fine healthy a constitution as I ever knew. Tell Anne this story, and kiss her for me, in presenting one of the inclosed caricatures. I put up several as Mrs. Randolph may have some of her family to whom they may give a moment's pleasure. My best affections are with Mr. Randolph and yourself. Adieu my dear.[96]

---

[96] "From Thomas Jefferson to Martha Jefferson Randolph, 4 August 1793," *Founders Online,* National Archives, last modified June 13, 2018, http://founders.archives.gov/documents/Jefferson/01-26-02-0558.

My dear Martha

Maria and I are scoring off the weeks which separate us from you. They wear off slowly, but time is sure tho' slow. Mr. D. Randolph left us three days ago. He went by the way of Presquisle and consequently will not enrapture Mrs. Randolph till the latter end of the month. I wrote to Mr. Randolph sometime ago to desire he would send off Tom Shackleford or Jupiter or any body else on the 1st. of September with the horse he has been so kind as to procure for me to meet at George town (at Shuter's tavern) a servant whom I shall send from hence on the same day with Tarquin, to exchange them, Tarquin to go to Monticello and the other come here to aid me in my journey. The messenger to ride a mule and lead the horse. I mention these things now, lest my letter should have miscarried. I received information yesterday of 500 bottles of wine arrived for me at Baltimore. I desired them to be sent to Richmond to Colo. Gamble to be forwarded to Monticello. They will be followed the next week with some things from hence. Should any waggons of the neighborhood be going down they might enquire for them. With the things sent from hence will go clothes for the servants to replace those sent last winter, which I did not conclude to be irrecoverably lost till Mr. Randolph's last letter. My blessings to your little ones, love to you all, and friendly how d-ye's to my good neighbors. Adieu. Your's affectionately

Th: Jefferson[97]

[97] "From Thomas Jefferson to Martha Jefferson Randolph, 18 August 1793," *Founders Online*, National Archives, last modified June 13, 2018, http://founders.archives.gov/documents/Jefferson/01-26-02-0638.

My Dear Martha

I received this day Mr. Randolph's letter of Aug. 31. with the horse, rather thin, having performed his journey in 7. days. However I shall hope to recruit him before I set out. The servant gives a very good account of him. The President sets out the day after tomorrow for Mount Vernon, and will be back about the last of the month. Within 4 or 5. days or a week after his return I can set out. The yellow fever, of which I wrote Mr. Randolph last week still encreases. The last week about twice as many have died as did the week before. I imagine there are between 3. and 400. persons ill of it. I propose after the President's departure to remove my office into the country so as to have no further occasion to go into the town. I was just about ordering some few stores to be got and sent off to Richmond for Monticello: but I think it too unsafe now, and shall therefore write to Colo. Gamble to send up some from Richmond.—Tell Mr. Randolph that the box for me in the Custom house at Bermuda must be a small Orrery, cost 2 ½ or 3 guineas.—If Mrs. Beverley Randolph is still with you tell her that the Indians having refused to meet our Commissioners, we expect Mr. Randolph her spousy1 here in the course of a week on his way back. Present my respects to her and your other friends with you. My best affections to Mr. Randolph, yourself and dear little ones. Adieu my dear dear Martha.

Th:J.[98]

98 "From Thomas Jefferson to Martha Jefferson Randolph, 8 September 1793," *Founders Online,* National Archives, last modified June 13, 2018, http://founders.archives.gov/documents/Jefferson/01-27-02-0060.

wrote, my dear Martha, by last week's post to Mr. Randolph. Yesterday I received his of Oct. 31. The fever in Philadelphia has almost entirely disappeared. The Physicians say they have no new infections since the great rains which have fallen. Some previous ones are still to die or recover, and so close this tragedy. I think however the Executive will remain here till the meeting of Congress, merely to furnish a rallying point to them. The refugee inhabitants are very generally returning into the city. Mr. T. Shippen and his lady are here. He is very slowly getting better. Still confined to the house. She well and very burly. I told her of her sister's pretensions to the fever and ague at Blenheim. She complained of receiving no letter. Tell this to Mrs. Carter, making it the subject of a visit express, which will be an act of good neighborhood.—The affairs of France are at present gloomy. Toulon has surrendered to England and Spain. So has Grand Anse and the country round about in St. Domingo. The English however have received a check before Dunkirk, probably a smart one, tho the particulars are not yet certainly known. I send Freneau's papers. He has discontinued them, but promises to resume again. I fear this cannot be till he has collected his arrearages. My best regards to Mr. Randolph. Accept my warmest love for yourself and Maria, compliments to Miss Jane, kisses to the children, friendly affections to all. Adieu Your's

Th: J.[99]

[99] "From Thomas Jefferson to Martha Jefferson Randolph, 10 November 1793," *Founders Online,* National Archives, last modified June 13, 2018, http://founders.archives.gov/documents/Jefferson/01-27-02-0309.

Philadelphia Dec. 1. 1793

My dear Martha

This place being entirely clear of all infection, the members of Congress are coming into it without fear. The President moved in yesterday, as did I also. I have got comfortably lodged at the corner of 7th. and Market street. —Dr. Waters is returned; not well, but better. Still always Hectic. He and Mrs. Waters are just gone to housekeeping for the first time. Mrs. Trist is also returned to town and means to take a small house and 3. or 4. boarders. Mr. Randolph, the Atty. Genl. having removed to German town during the fever, proposes not to return again to live in the city. Mrs. Washington is not yet returned.—So much for small news. As to great, we can only perceive in general that the French are triumphing in every quarter. They suffered a check as is said by the D. of Brunswick, losing about 2000. men, but this is nothing to their numerous victories. The account of the recapture of Toulon comes so many ways that we think it may now be believed.—St. Domingo has expelled all it's whites, has given freedom to all it's blacks, has established a regular government of the blacks and coloured people, and seems now to have taken it's ultimate form, and that to which all of the West India islands must come. The English have possession of two ports in the island, but acting professedly as the patrons of the whites, there is no danger of their gaining ground.— Freneau's and Fenno's papers are both put down for ever. My best affection to Mr. Randolph, Maria and friends. Kisses to the little ones. Adieu affectionately

Th: J.[100]

---

[100] "From Thomas Jefferson to Martha Jefferson Randolph, 1 December 1793," *Founders Online,* National Archives, last modified June 13, 2018, http://founders.archives.gov/documents/Jefferson/01-27-02-0437.

My dear Martha

In my letter of this day fortnight to Mr. Randolph, and that of this day week to Maria, I mentioned my wish that my horses might meet me at Fredericksburg on the 12th. of January. I now repeat it, lest those letters should miscarry. The President made yesterday, what I hope will be the last set at me to continue; but in this I am now immoveable, by any considerations whatever. My books and remains of furniture embark tomorrow for Richmond. There will be as much in bulk as what went before. I think to address them to Colo. Gamble. As I retained longest here the things most necessary, they are of course those I shall want soonest when I get home. Therefore I would wish them, after their arrival to be carried up in preference to the packages formerly sent. The Nos. most wanting will begin at 67.—I hope that by the next post I shall be able to send Mr. Randolph a printed copy of our correspondence with Mr. Genet and Mr. Hammond, as communicated to Congress. They are now in the press. Our affairs with England and Spain have a turbid appearance. The letting loose the Algerines on us, which has been contrived by England, has produced peculiar irritation. I think Congress will indemnify themselves by high duties on all articles of British importation. If this should produce war, tho not wished for, it seems not to be feared. My best affections to Mr. Randolph, Maria, and our friends with you. Kisses to the little ones. Adieu my dear Martha. Your's with all love

Th: Jefferson[101]

---

[101] "From Thomas Jefferson to Martha Jefferson Randolph, 22 December 1793," *Founders Online,* National Archives, last modified June 13, 2018, http://founders.archives.gov/documents/Jefferson/01-27-02-0536.

Thomas Jefferson as Vice President

1797 - 1801

Thomas Jefferson ran for President when George Washington didn't run for a third term. Thomas ran against John Adams, and subsequently lost the election, and became Vice President.

The years prior Patsy had three more children, Ellen Wayles Randolph, who died young, and the second was another daughter who would be gifted the same name, but she would survive. She would have one more daughter during this time, Cornelia Jefferson Randolph.

***

Without further ado,
The letters of Thomas and Patsy,
During Thomas Jefferson's time as Vice President

My dear Martha

I wrote to Mr. Randolph two or three days ago, but I imagine he will recieve the letter at Richmond on his way up: for we expect he will of course come up this week. He has a more dangerous competitor in Billy Wood than had arisen before. But I hear little about it. I arrived in good health at home this day sennight. The mountain had then been in bloom ten days. I find that the natural productions of the spring are about a fortnight earlier here than at Fredericksburg. But where art and attention can do any thing, some one in a large collection of inhabitants, as in a town, will be before ordinary individuals whether of town or country. I have heard of you but once since I left home, and am impatient to know that you are all well. I have however so much confidence in the dose of health with which Monticello charges you in summer and autumn that I count on it's carrying you well through the winter. The difference between the health enjoyed at Varina and Presqu'isle is merely the effect of this. Therefore do not ascribe it to Varina and stay there too long. The bloom of Monticello is chilled by my solitude. It makes me wish the more that yourself and sister were here to enjoy it. I value the enjoiments of this life only in proportion as you participate them with me. All other attachments are weakening, and I approach the state of mind when nothing will hold me here but my love for yourself and sister and the tender connections you have added to me. I hope you will write to me: as nothing is so pleasing during your absence as these proofs of your love. Be assured my dear daughter that you possess mine in it's utmost limits. Kiss the dear little ones for me. I wish we had one of them here. Adieu affectionately.

I inclose you a letter I received in Philadelphia from Mde. Salimberi. As I came in a stage it was impossible to accomodate her. I wrote her the fact with such friendly expressions for us all as might tend to prevent her imputing it to unwillingness. Had it not been for the unroofing our house, I would have invited her to come here and spend the summer with you.[102]

[102] "From Thomas Jefferson to Martha Jefferson Randolph, 27 March 1797," *Founders Online,* National Archives, last modified June 13, 2018, http://founders.archives.gov/documents/Jefferson/01-29-02-0260.

Varina March 31st. 1797

My Dearest Father

The first certain accounts we had of your arrival were conveyed by your letter to Mr. Randolph which would as you suposed have met on his way up had we not previously determined upon having the children innoculated. But every circumstance of season health &c. conspiring to make the present opportunity favorable Mr. Randolph thought no interest of his could excuse his letting it slip. I have often experienced that a mother's heart was of all things in nature the least subject to reason but never more fully than at present. The idea of exposing my children to such a disorder with out being able to accompany them alltho I have the certainty of their finding in their Father as tender and an infinitely more skill full nurse than my self, makes me perfectly miserable. I never look at them but my eyes fill with tears to think how soon we shall part and *perhaps* for ever. The anxiety I feel on their account my Dear Father does not prevent my feeling most sensibly for the solitude and gloom of your present situation. I never take a view of your solitary fire side but my heart swells. However as nothing detains us now but the children I hope soon be restored to your paternal embraces and dispel by the presence of your children the cloud which obscures the beauties of spring, no where so enchanting as at Monticello. My Sister joins me the tenderest love. As the boys are waiting I am obliged to conclude with Dearest Father your most affectionate

M. Randolph[103]

[103] "To Thomas Jefferson from Martha Jefferson Randolph, 31 March 1797," *Founders Online,* National Archives, last modified June 13, 2018, http://founders.archives.gov/documents/Jefferson/01-29-02-0265.

Dear Sir

I recieved yours my dear Martha, of Mar. 31. four days ago. The inoculation at Richmond having stopped that post I send this by the way of Fredsbg. I entirely approve of your resolution to have the children inoculated. I had before been so much convinced of the expediency of the measure that I had taken it for granted before your letter informed me of it. I am called to Philadelphia to a meeting of Congress the 15th. of May and shall leave Monticello the 3d. or 4th. of that month. As Mr. Randolph informs me you would have quitted Varina and come up the beginning of this month but for the inoculation, would it not be best for you as soon as the children are quite recovered from the disease, to come up, you, Maria and Ellen and send the carriage back for Mr. Randolph and the children. In this way I shall have the pleasure of seeing you certainly and him and the children probably before my departure and can make better arrangements for your accomodation during my absence. Still however let all this depend on your convenience. My love to Maria. Tell her I have made a new law, which is only *to answer letters*. It would have been her turn to have recieved a letter had she not lost it by not writing. Adieu most affectionately both of you.[104]

---

[104] "From Thomas Jefferson to Martha Jefferson Randolph, 9 April 1797," *Founders Online,* National Archives, last modified June 13, 2018, http://founders.archives.gov/documents/Jefferson/01-29-02-0274.

My dear Martha

I arrived here in good health on the 7th. day after my departure from home, without any intervening accident and am as well as when I left home. I recieved here the inclosed letter from Mr. Pintard our Consul at Madeira who sais it was given him by one of your old convent acquaintances settled there. I suppose the letter will inform you of more particulars. We yesterday recieved the President's speech. Till the answer shall be given in we cannot judge what work the legislature will now take in hand, nor consequently how long we shall be here. Opinions vary from 4. to 6. weeks. My next letter will give a better idea of the time of my return which will be within a week after the rising of Congress. Our affairs with France become more and more gloomy. Those of England every day more desperate. Nothing but their desperation prevents the stronger party in our government from making common cause with them. Prices of produce are at a stand. The current price of James river tobacco is 9. dollars. This information may be desireable to some of our mercantile neighbors. My love to my dear Maria. I write to Mr. Randolph on the presumption he is at Richmond. My affections are with yourself and Maria and my wishes to be with you. Continue to love me. Adieu.[105]

---

[105] "From Thomas Jefferson to Martha Jefferson Randolph, 18 May 1797," *Founders Online,* National Archives, last modified June 13, 2018, http://founders.archives.gov/documents/Jefferson/01-29-02-0298.

My dear Martha

Yours of May 20 came to hand the 1st. inst. I imagine you recieved mine of May 18. about six days after the date of yours. It was written the first post-day after my arrival here. The commission you inclosed for Maria is executed, and the things are in the care of Mr. Boyce of Richmond, who is returning from hence with some goods of his own, and will deliver them to Mr. Johnston.—I recieve with inexpressible pleasure the information your letter contained. After your own happy establishment, which has given me an inestimable friend to whom I can leave the care of every thing I love, the only anxiety I had remaining was to see Maria also so associated as to ensure her happiness. She could not have been more so to my wishes, if I had had the whole earth free to have chosen a partner for her. I now see our fireside formed into a groupe, no one member of which has a fibre in their composition which can ever produce any jarring or jealousies among us. No irregular passions, no dangerous bias, which may render problematical the future fortunes and happiness of our descendants. We are quieted as to their condition for at least one generation more. In order to keep us all together, instead of a present provision in Bedford, as in your case, I think to open and resettle the plantation of Pantops for them. When I look to the ineffable pleasures of my family society, I become more and more disgusted with the jealousies, the hatred, and the rancorous and malignant passions of this scene, and lament my having ever again been drawn into public view. Tranquility is now my object. I have seen enough of political honors to know that they are but splendid torments: and however one might be disposed to render services on which any of their fellow citizens should set a value; yet when as many would deprecate them as a public calamity, one may well entertain a modest doubt of their real importance, and feel the impulse of duty to be very weak. The real difficulty is that being once delivered into the hands of others, whose

154

feelings are friendly to the individual and warm to the public cause, how to withdraw from them without leaving a dissatisfaction in their mind and an impression of pusillanimity with the public.

Congress, in all probability will rise on Saturday the 17th. inst. the day after you will recieve this. I shall leave Philadelphia Monday the 19th. pass a day at Georgetown and a day at Fredericksburg, at which place I wish my *chair* and horses to be Sunday evening the 25th. Of course they must set out Saturday morning the 24th. This gives me the chance of another post, as you will, the evening before that, recieve by the post a letter of a week later date than this, so that if any thing should happen within a week to delay the rising of Congress, I may still notify it and change the time of the departure of my horses. Jupiter must pursue the rout by Noel's to which he will come the first day, and by Chew's to Fredericksburg the next. I fix his rout because were any accident to get me along earlier, or him later, we might meet on the road. Not yet informed that Mr. Randolph is returned I have thought it safest to commit this article to my letter to you. The news of the day I shall write to him. My warmest love to yourself and Maria. Adieu affectionately.

Th: Jefferson[106]

[106] "From Thomas Jefferson to Martha Jefferson Randolph, 8 June 1797," *Founders Online,* National Archives, last modified June 13, 2018, http://founders.archives.gov/documents/Jefferson/01-29-02-0333.

My dear Martha

I am at length got well of a terrible cold, which I think must have proceeded from the intense cold of the day I left Belmont. It became very bad by the time I got to Baltimore, and has been worse here. However it is now entirely passed off. We are here lounging our time away, doing nothing, and having nothing to do. It gives me great regret to be passing my time so uselessly when it could have been so importantly employed at home. I cannot but believe that we shall become ashamed of staying here, and go home in February or March at furthest. Nor are we relieved by the pleasures of society here. For partly from bankruptcies partly from party dissensions society is torn up by the roots. I envy those who stay at home, enjoying the society of their friendly neighbors, blessed with their firesides, and employed in doing something every day which looks usefully to futurity. I expect you will of course charge me before my departure with the procuring you such articles of convenience here as you can get best here. I shall be sending some things for myself in the spring. Tell Mr. Randolph I shall be glad from time to time to exchange meteorological diaries with him, that we may have a comparative view of the climates of this place and ours. I received a letter from Maria last week. She had got quite well of her sprain and was then at the Chesnut grove. However I suppose you hear from one another more directly than through me. Let me also hear from you, as your welfare, Mr. Randolph's and the little ones are the things nearest my heart. Do not let them forget me. Adieu my dear Martha affectionately.[107]

---

[107] "From Thomas Jefferson to Martha Jefferson Randolph, 27 December 1797," *Founders Online,* National Archives, last modified June 13, 2018, http://founders.archives.gov/documents/Jefferson/01-29-02-0480.

Jupiter had given us so terrible an account of your sufferings from the ice on the patowmac that we began to be seriously alarmed about you, before the arrival of your letters, which came both to gether; it was with infinite pleasure than that we learned you had got the better of your cold and were at least *comfortably* if not agreably fixed for the winter. it is much more than we can boast of, for the extreme dampness of the situation and an absolute want of offices of every kind to shelter the servants whilst in the performance of their duties, have occasioned more sickness than I ever saw in a family in my life. pleurisie, rhumatism, and every disorder proceeding from cold have been so frequent that we have scarcely had at any one time *well* enough to tend the sick—our intercourse with Monticello has been allmost *daily* they have been generally well there except Tom and Goliah who are both *about* again and poor little Harriot who died a few days after you left us. I shall joyfully accept of the offer you make of executing my comissions in Philadelphia. Mr Randolph has some money remaining in Barnes's hands which I should be extremely obliged to you to lay out in plate, table spoons tea spoons &c as far as it will go. I imagine there is enough of it for that purpose and as much (considering the many other urgent calls for money building will occasion) as will be convenient to bestow upon that article. and if such a thing is to be had *a game of the goose* it was a promise made to the children which Richmond does not furnish the means of paying. I look forward with great impatience to March I am afraid to flatter my self with the prospect of seeing you sooner and I feel every day more strongly the impossibility of becoming habituated to your absence—sepparated in my infancy from every other friend, and accustomed to look up to you alone, every sentiment of tenderness my nature was susceptible of was for many years centered in you, and no connexion formed since that could weaken a sentiment interwoven with my very existence. I have heard from Maria thru Mr Eppes she deals much in promises but very little in deeds that are to be performed with a pen she was in as good health and better spirits than usual adieu my dearest Father the children unanimously join in love to you and believe me with every sentiment of tenderness gratitude and respect your affectionate child—

M. Randolph[108]

---

[108] "To Thomas Jefferson from Martha Jefferson Randolph, 22 January 1798," *Founders Online,* National Archives, last modified June 13, 2018, http://founders.archives.gov/documents/Jefferson/01-30-02-0028.

I ought oftener, my dear Martha, to recieve your letters, for the very great pleasure they give me, & especially when they express your affections for me. for though I cannot doubt them, yet they are among those truths which tho' not doubted we love to hear repeated. here too they serve like gleams of light, to chear a dreary scene, where envy, hatred, malice, revenge, & all the worst passions of men are marshalled to make one another as miserable as possible. I turn from this with pleasure to contrast it with your fire side, where the single evening I passed at it was worth more than ages here. indeed I feel myself detaching very fast, perhaps too fast, from every thing but yourself, your sister, & those who are identified with you. these form the last hold the world will have on me, the cords which will be cut only when I am loosened from this state of being. I am looking forward to the spring with all the fondness of desire to meet you all once more, and with the change of season, to enjoy also a change of scene & of society. yet the time of our leaving this is not yet talked of. I am much concerned to hear the state of health of mr Randolph & the family, mentioned in your letters of Jan. 22. & 28. surely, my dear, it would be better for you to remove to Monticello. the south pavillion the Parlour & Study, will accomodate your family; & I should think mr Randolph would find less inconvenience in the riding it would occasion him than in the loss of his own & his family's health. let me beseech you then to go there, and to use every thing & every body as if I were there. if mr Randolph will take on himself to command the usual functions of the servants, carts, waggon, and other resources of the place, you may make yourselves comfortable there. I shall anxiously hope to hear that you adopt this plan. I wrote to mr Randolph on the subject of a rider for our Fredericksburg post who may be relied on. the proposition should be here, if any one will undertake it, by the 14th. inst. but the postmaster has promised to keep it open a little longer. £100. Virginia money will be given, if the person be approvedly trustworthy.—all your commissions shall be executed, not forgetting the game of the goose, if we can find out what it is; for there is some difficulty in that. kiss all the little ones for me: present me affectionately to mr Randolph, & my warmest love to yourself. Adieu.[109]

---

[109] "From Thomas Jefferson to Martha Jefferson Randolph, 8 February 1798," *Founders Online,* National Archives, last modified June 13, 2018, http://founders.archives.gov/documents/Jefferson/01-30-02-0061.

You tell me My dear Father that I ought to write oftener and enforce your request with an argument that has allways been irresistable with me "the pleasure it gives you" but the expression of a tenderness like mine is not easily rendered even by those endowed with the happy faculty of expressing their feelings. that fortunate gift however was never mine or else subjects for a letter could never fail while the heart that dictates them continued to beat, but there is so little consonance between the cold & inadequate language of a pen totally unversed in the art of describing them, and the glowing affections of a heart fraught with every tender sentiment the human mind is susceptible of, that I never can bear the weak and imperfect picture of my feelings which a letter presents. the solitude in which we live affords little else to comunicate but the sensations and reflections of its inhabitants. our dwelling begins to be infinitely more comfortable by the addition and repairs of some offices and the arrival of our furniture from Varina perhaps allso having acquired a seasoning to the place, added to this Mr Randolph has taken all his workmen, wheel rights carpenters smiths &c under his own command which renders his presence indispensibly necessary here, and of course the acceptance of your attentive and affectionate offer impracticable. Isaac has given him a great deal of trouble allways dissatisfied and rebellious he at last eloped with an intention of going to Eppington but being twice taken by the patrol and escaping both times he returned home much humbled and apparently better disposed to work. my communications with John have been regular from the first of January according to the little callender you left me. your smoke house was under mined and seventeen pieces of meat taken out the same accident happened at Dunlora about the same time and by the same means tho the loss they sustained was less rather than yours you have hardly I imagine been informed of poor Aunt Skipwith's death she had been perfectly insane for two months before it, tho well otherwise. she expired in a fit with out ever having had an interval of reason or knowing any one about her. we have Mr & Mrs P. Carr & their family with us at present consisting of his Sister & 2 children; of Browse we have not heard a word but by your letters. Mr Randolphs accompts as Executor guardian &c have prevented his writing to you this post but the next he will certainly do it and give you the information you demand respecting your affairs, Davenport's particularly who I fear has done little or nothing this winter this however is rather conjecture than any certain knowledge. we are all in perfect health but Ellen who looks wretchedly but I hope it is the effect of teething only adieu my Dear Papa I am afraid you will scarcely be able to decypher this scrawl, written within the noise and confusion of the children and chat of the Ladies believe me with unchangeable and truly ardent affection yours

M Randolph[110]

[110] "To Thomas Jefferson from Martha Jefferson Randolph, 26 February 1798," *Founders Online,* National Archives, last modified June 13, 2018, http://founders.archives.gov/documents/Jefferson/01-30-02-0095.

Mr. Randolph's letter of Mar. 26. informs me you are all well at Belmont. my last news from Eppington was of Mar. 20. when all were well there. I have myself had remarkeably good health through the winter, since the cold which I took on my way here. the advance of the season makes me long to get home. the first shad we had here was Mar. 16. and Mar. 28. was the first day we could observe a greenish hue on the weeping willow from it's young leaves. not the smallest symptom of blossoming yet on any species of fruit tree. all this proves that we have near two months in the year of vegetable life, and of animal happiness so far as they are connected, more in our canton than here. the issue of a debate now before the H. of Representatives will enable us to judge of the time of adjournment. but it will be some days before the issue is known. in the mean time they talk of the last of this month. letters by a late arrival from France give reason to believe they do not mean to declare war against us; but that they mean to destroy British commerce with all nations, neutral as well as belligerent. to this the Swedes & Danes submit, and so must we unless we prefer war. a letter from mr Short informs me of the death of the old Dutchess Danville. he talks of coming in this spring or summer. I have purchased an excellent harpsichord for Maria, which I hope is by this time arrived at Monticello, with a box of trees to which I asked mr Randolph's attention by the last post. among these were cranberries, raspberries & strawberries of great value. I am afflicted with the difficulty of procuring horses for the farm, or rather for the waggon in place of the mules to be turned over to the farm, which is a good idea. I am afflicted too with the fear that the roof of the house is not going on as my necessities require. I have engaged a fine housejoiner here to go on with me. my most friendly salutations to mr Randolph & tenderest love to yourself and the little ones. Adieu affectionately.[111]

[111] "From Thomas Jefferson to Martha Jefferson Randolph, 5 April 1798," *Founders Online,* National Archives, last modified June 13, 2018, http://founders.archives.gov/documents/Jefferson/01-30-02-0169.

Dearest Father

Nothing makes me feel your absence so sensibly as the beauty of the season; when every object in nature invites one into the fields, the close monotonous streets of a city which offers no charms of society with in doors to compensate for the dreariness of the scene with out, must be absolutely intolerable: particularly to you who have such interesting employment at home. Monticello shines with a transcendent luxury of vegetation above the rest of the neighbourhood as yet, we have been entirely supplied with vegetables from there having no sort of a garden here nor any prospect of one this year. I am glad to have it in my power to give you a more favorable account of things than Mr Randolph did in his last which was written immediately after a frost that blasted every appearance of vegetation, but John informs me alltho the peaches cherries (except the kentish) and figs which had been uncovered were gone past recovery for *this* year, yet of strawberries, raspberries, currants &c &c &c there will be more than common—I dined at Monticello a fortnight ago and saw Maria's harpsichord which arrived safe except the lock and 1 or 2 pieces of the moulding which got torn off some way. it is a charming one I think tho certainly inferior to mine. you have probably not heard of the death of poor Aunt Fleming, that of Mrs. Archer (Polly Bolling that was) is still more recent it took place at her Father's house a few weeks since. we have been all well but Jefferson who had declined rapidly for some time from a disorder which had baffled every attention and change of diet, the only remedy we ventured to try; but Mr Sneed opening school and Jeffy being hurried out of bed every morning at sunrise and obliged after a breakfast of bread and milk to walk 2 miles to school: his spirits returned his complexion cleared up and I am in hopes that his disorder has left him entirely. he is much mended in appearance strength & spirits, which had been low to an alarming degree—Anne Just begins to read and little Ellen

165

points at grand Papa's picture over the chimney when ever she is asked where he is. adieu my dearest Father blest as I am in my family you are still wanting to compleat my happiness. Monticello will be interesting indeed when with the prospect of it the loved idea of yourself and Dear Maria will be so intimately blended as they will in a few weeks I hope, once more adieu and believe me with every sentiment of affection yours

M Randolph[112]

[112] "To Thomas Jefferson from Martha Jefferson Randolph, 12 May 1798," *Founders Online,* National Archives, last modified June 13, 2018, http://founders.archives.gov/documents/Jefferson/01-30-02-0243.

My dear Martha

Having nothing of business to write on to mr Randolph this week I with pleasure take up my pen to express all my love to you, and my wishes once more to find myself in the only scene where, for me, the sweeter affections of life have any exercise. but when I shall be with you seems still uncertain. we have been so long looking forward from 3. weeks to 3. weeks, & always with disappointment, that I know not now what to expect. I shall immediately write to Maria & recommend to mr Eppes and her to go up to Monticello as soon as my stores, which went from here a week ago, shall be sent on from Richmond; because our groceries &c. were pretty well exhausted when I left home. these may well arrive at Richmond by about the 20th. instant, so that if my recommendation is adopted they may be soon with you, and contribute some variety to your scene. for you to feel all the happiness of your quiet situation, you should know the rancorous passions which tear every breast here, even of the sex which should be a stranger to them. politics & party hatreds destroy the happiness of every being here. they seem, like salamanders, to consider fire as their element. I am in hopes you make free use of the garden & any other resources at Monticello. the children I am afraid will have forgotten me. however my memory may perhaps be hung on the game of the goose which I am to carry them. kiss them for me, and present me affectionately to mr Randolph. to yourself my tenderest love & Adieu.

Th: Jefferson

P.S. since writing the above, Richardson has called on me. he has recieved a letter from mr Duke expressing doubts whether he shall be able to go & do mr Randolph's work. he has therefore determined to leave this place in the first vessel, and you may expect him in 3. or 4. weeks to be with you ready for work, & much improved, from what he has seen & done here.[113]

[113] "From Thomas Jefferson to Martha Jefferson Randolph, 17 May 1798," *Founders Online,* National Archives, last modified June 13, 2018, http://founders.archives.gov/documents/Jefferson/01-30-02-0251.

My dear Martha

My letter by the last post was to mr Randolph, dated May 24. yours of the 12th. inst. did not get to hand till the 29th. so it must have laid by a post somewhere. the receipt of it, by kindling up all my recollections increases my impatience to leave this place & every thing which can be disgusting, for Monticello and my dear family, comprising every thing which is pleasurable to me in this world. it has been proposed in Congress to adjourn on the 14th. of June. I have little expectation of it myself: but whatever be their determination, I am determined myself; and my letter of next week will probably bring orders for my horses. Jupiter should therefore be in readiness to depart on a night's warning, with three horses, as a workman accompanies me from here. it will be necessary also to send for my letter to the post office the evening of it's arrival, or rather to order him to attend the arrival of the post at Milton, & carry the letters to Belmont to recieve his orders if any. some think Congress will wait here till their envoys return from France, for whom a vessel was sent the 1st. of April, so that they may be here the 2d week of July. others think they will not adjourn at all, as they have past a bill for capturing French armed vessels found near our coast, which is pretty generally considered as a commencement of war without a declaration. so that we consider war as no longer doubtful. Volney & a ship load of others of his nation will sail from hence on Sunday. another ship load will go in about 3. weeks. a bill is now brought in to suspend all communication with France & her dominions: and we expect another to declare our treaty with her void. mr Randolph will percieve that this certainty of war must decide the objects of our husbandry to be such as will keep to the end of it.—I am sorry to hear of Jefferson's indisposition, but glad you do not physic him. this leaves nature free and unembarrassed in her own tendencies to repair what is wrong. I hope to hear or to find that he is recovered. kiss them all for me. remember me affectionately to mr Randolph and be assured yourself of my constant & tenderest love. Adieu.

Th: Jefferson

P.S. it would be well that Davenport should be immediately informed that I am coming home. since writing this I have recieved a letter from mr Eppes, informing me that all are well there. he & Maria will set out for Monticello June 20th.[114]

---

[114] "From Thomas Jefferson to Martha Jefferson Randolph, 31 May 1798," *Founders Online,* National Archives, last modified June 13, 2018, http://founders.archives.gov/documents/Jefferson/01-30-02-0271.

Wednesday. Aug. 15. 98.

Th:J. to his dear Martha.

Ellen appeared to be feverish the evening you went away: but visiting her a little before I went to bed, I found her quite clear of fever, & was convinced the quickness of pulse which had alarmed me had proceeded from her having been in uncommon spirits and been constantly running about the house through the day & especially in the afternoon. since that she has had no symptom of fever, and is otherwise better than when you left her. the girls indeed suppose she had a little fever last night, but I am sure she had not, as she was well at 8. aclock in the evening & very well in the morning, and they say she slept soundly through the night. they judged only from her breathing. every body else is well: and only wishing to see you. I am persecuted with questions 'when I think you will come'? my respects to mr & mrs Carter & affectionate salutations to our more particular friends. if you set out home after dinner be sure to get off between four & five. Adieu my dear.[115]

[115] "From Thomas Jefferson to Martha Jefferson Randolph, 15 August 1798," *Founders Online,* National Archives, last modified June 13, 2018, http://founders.archives.gov/documents/Jefferson/01-30-02-0345.

My dear Martha

I reached Fredericksburg the day after I left you, and this place on Christmas-day, having (thanks to my pelisse) felt no more sensation of cold on the road than if I had been in a warm bed. nevertheless I got a small cold which brought on an inflammation in the eyes, head ach &c so that I kept within doors yesterday & only took my seat in Senate to-day. I have as yet had little opportunity of hearing news; I only observe in general that the republican gentlemen whom I have seen consider the state of the public mind to be fast advancing in their favor. whether their opponents will push for war or not is not yet developed. no business is as yet brought into the Senate, & very little into the other house: so that I was here in good time. I shall be at a loss how to direct to you hereafter, uncertain as I am whether you will leave home & where you will be. on this subject you must inform me. present me affectionately to mr Randolph, and kiss all the little ones for me, not forgetting *Elleanoroon.* be assured yourself of my constant and tender love. Adieu my ever dear Martha.[116]

---

[116] "From Thomas Jefferson to Martha Jefferson Randolph, 27 December 1798," *Founders Online,* National Archives, last modified June 13, 2018, http://founders.archives.gov/documents/Jefferson/01-30-02-0413.

Philadelphia Jan. 23. 99.

The object of this letter, my very dear Martha, is merely to inform you I am well, and to convey to you the expressions of my love. it will not be new to tell you that your letters do not come as often as I could wish. I have not heard from Albemarle or Chesterfield since I left home, now 5. weeks. this deprives me of the gleams of pleasure wanting to relieve the dreariness of this scene, where not one single occurrence is calculated to produce pleasing sensations. tho' I hear not from you, I hope you are all well, and that the little ones, even Ellen talk of me sometimes. if your visit to Goochland has been relinquished as I expect, I shall hope to find you on my return still at Monticello. within a post or two I shall announce to you the day for my cavalry to be sent off. in the mean time I feed myself with the pleasure which the approach of that day always gives me. I hope you will aid John in his preparations in the garden. I have heard nothing from mr Richardson about the hiring of labourers & consequently am anxious about my summer operations. Dr. Bache will set out for our neighborhood next month. I have persuaded mrs Bache to let him go first and prepare a *gite*. in the mean time they are packing their furniture. let George know that the nail rod sent from here in December has, with the vessel in which it was, been cast away at sea; and that another supply was shipped here two or three days ago, and will probably be at Richmond about the 10th. of February. present me affectionately to mr Randolph to whom I inclose Gerry's correspondence & Pickering's report. kiss all the little ones, and recieve the tender and unmingled effusions of my love to yourself. Adieu

Th: Jefferson[117]

---

[117] "From Thomas Jefferson to Martha Jefferson Randolph, 23 January 1799," *Founders Online,* National Archives, last modified June 13, 2018, http://founders.archives.gov/documents/Jefferson/01-30-02-0443.

My dear Martha

I wrote to mr Randolph on the 30th. of Jan. having just then recieved his of the 19th. it was not till yesterday that I learned from the Post office that our post now departs on Wednesday morning from this place. my letters hitherto have been written for Thursday morning, so that you will have recieved them a week later. tell mr Randolph that the day on which I wrote to him, but after I had sealed my letter, a bill was brought in to raise 30. regiments of infantry cavalry & artillery, on the event of an invasion or in case of imminent danger of invasion in the opinion of the President. regiments are now proposed to be about 1000. our land army will then be the *existing* army 5000. the additional army 9000, this *eventual* army 30,000. (instead of the Provisional one of 10,000 the act for which is expired) and the *volunteer army*, which is now to be formed into brigades & divisions & to be exercised. we have no particular information as to the price of tobo. but generally that that as well as all other produce is higher in England than ever known. the immense quantities of paper which their circumstances have forced them to create are now sensibly felt in the enlivening effect which always takes place in the first moment in the delusive shape of prosperity. they are accordingly now singing Hosannas for the unparalleled rise of their finances, & manufactures. we shall catch a little of the benefit in the beginning as their paper money price for tobo. will be hard money to us. but it will soon be fetched up as their paper money price for manufactures will be a hard money price to us. we ought to prepare against being involved in their embarassments by setting in by times to domestic manufacture.—Jupiter with my horses must be at Fredericksburg on Tuesday evening the 5th. of March. I shall leave this place on the 1st. or 2d. you will recieve this the 14th. inst. I am already lighthearted at the approach of my departure. kiss my dear children for me.

nexpressible love to yourself & the sincerest affection to mr Randolph. Adieu.[118]

---

[118] "From Thomas Jefferson to Martha Jefferson Randolph, 5 February 1799," *Founders Online,* National Archives, last modified June 13, 2018, http://founders.archives.gov/documents/Jefferson/01-31-02-0006.

I am ashamed indeed my Dearest Father to have so *justly* incurred the reproach contained in your last. allthough the trip down the country was soon relinquished, yet my time has been more varied than is usual with me; after your departure we spent ten days with Mrs Divers, Carr, Trist, &c &c &c during which time I went to a ball in Charlottesville, *danced* at it and returned home fatigued and unwell to prepare for our return to Bellmont; where for the consideration of 20£ Allen consented to let us remain till the fifteenth of March. this will give Mr Randolph time, at least to empty a barn for the reception of our furniture. the visit from Mrs Jefferson with preparations for a second ball where I accompanied her and the girls, added to the cares of the household some what encreased by so long an absence from them, will account in some measure for the neglect of so sacred and agreable a duty—John has been once only to recieve orders about the garden; his excuse was the negligence of Phil in furnishing but one load of manure, the want of which he seemed to think rendered his attentions useless. Mr Randolph will give you the details of the farm which he has visited twice during your absence, and the newspapers have informed you of the loss the friends of Liberty have in the death of young Thomson of Petersburg; which is the only event of any consequence that has taken place since you left us—for the rest, every thing stands as you left it, even your house. Davenport has I am afraid sold the plank he engaged to furnish for it, at least McGehee told Mr Randolph so, and he has certainly agreed to furnish some one in Milton with plank immediately. Mr Randolph has some thoughts of employing a young man who has engaged to work for him (an acquaintance and reccommended by McGehee) to do it if Davenport delays any longer. the children all join in tender love to you, from Virginia to *Annin Yoon* who speaks much of you, and as a constant resource against *ill treatment* from her Papa and my self;

whom she frequently threatens with going to *Phil delphy* she sends her love to you and begs you will bring her a *cake*—I must beg the favour of you to bring for Jefferson the *newest* edition of Sandford and Merton the old editions consisting of two volumes are to be had in Richmond but as we have heard there is a third & perhaps fourth volume come out which are not to be met with there, I must apply to you to acquit my word with him. since I began to write we have been informed that Davenport has this very day set about your work

Mr Randolph finds it impossible to write by this post but bids me tell you the tobacco is just prized (13 hogsheads in all) and by the next post he will give you the details of the other operations of the farm. adieu Dearest Father I write in the midst of the noise of the children and particularly your little *seet heart* who has interrupted me so often that I have scarcely been able to connect one sentence with another. believe me with tenderest reverence and affection yours unchangeably

M. Randolph[119]

---

[119] "To Thomas Jefferson from Martha Jefferson Randolph, 8 February 1799," *Founders Online,* National Archives, last modified June 13, 2018, http://founders.archives.gov/documents/Jefferson/01-31-02-0013.

Uncertain whether this will still find you at Philadelphia or no, I shall write but a few lines; happy in the thought of it's being the last Time I shall have it in my power to do so, before we embrace you. I have heard from Maria since the letter I recieved from you containing an account of her indisposition and recovery, and Mr Eppes mentioned that she had been again unwell, too much so to go to Mnt Blanc the appointed day. I have not heard from her since by which I hope it has not proved serious. your tobacco is not gone down yet, George (smith) continues *ill* confined in Milton and some of the others are unwell, I do not recollect who but Mr Randolph has been over several times lately so I suppose they have not suffered. adieu Dearest Father your return is the favorite theme of us all, even little Ellen talks incessantly of you & I am certain she will know you, for she speaks with great tenderness of you, more, than she would of a person she did not remember, and Love. her constant message is to come home and bring her a cake. adieu once more believe me with tenderness unspeakable your affectionate child

M. Randolph[120]

---

[120] "To Thomas Jefferson from Martha Jefferson Randolph, 22 February 1799," *Founders Online,* National Archives, last modified June 13, 2018, http://founders.archives.gov/documents/Jefferson/01-31-02-0036.

My dear Martha

I wrote on the 13th. inst. to mr Randolph. I now inclose you a letter from your friend Mde. Salimberi. it came under cover to me. and without looking at the second cover, or suspecting it not for me, I broke the seal, a few words in the beginning shewed me it was not, & on looking at the back I found it was addressed to you.—M. Bureau-Pusy, the companion of la Fayette, with his family & Mde. Dupont arrived at N. York some time ago. Dupont, with his son (late consul) & family arrived there a few days ago. I have a letter from La Fayette in which he says he should sail for America in July, but as he also expressed a wish to see the event of our negociation I suppose he will not come till reconciliation is established by that. J. Randolph's affair is not over. a rancorous report was made to the H. of R. yesterday by a committee. it would seem as if the army themselves were to hew down whoever shall propose to reduce them. the non-intercourse law is to be renewed, but whether only for the tobacco states, or for all, is a question. were it not for the prospect of it's expiring by the effect of a treaty, our state would do better to drop the culture of tobo. altogether.—I am made happy by a letter from mr Eppes, recd two or three days ago & informing me that Maria was become a mother & was well. it was written the day after the event. these circumstances are balm to the painful sensations of this place. I look forward with hope to the moment when we are all to be reunited again. it is proposed that we shall adjourn about the middle of March; & as the proposition comes from the Eastern members it will probably prevail. there is really nothing to do but to authorize them to make up their deficit of 5. millions by borrowing at 8. or 10. per cent. my friend Govr. Rutledge of S. Carolina is dead. news is this moment recieved here of the death of Govr. Mifflin at Lancaster; and there is a rumor of the death of George the 3d. the great & antient house of Cuningham & Nesbitt of this place has stopped paiment. it is but the beginning of a great crush. no commerce was more deeply interested than our's in the deposits at Hamburgh. indeed our commerce & navigation generally are in a state of prostration. I am anxious as you may suppose to hear from you, having heard nothing since I left home. I hope you all continue well, yet should be happier to know it. I inclose a little tale for Anne. to Ellen you must make big promises, which I know a bit of gingerbread will pay off. kiss them all for me. my affectionate salutations to mr Randolph & tender & unceasing love to yourself. Adieu my ever dear Martha affectionately.

Th: Jefferson[121]

[121] "From Thomas Jefferson to Martha Jefferson Randolph, 21 January 1800," *Founders Online,* National Archives, last modified June 13, 2018, http://founders.archives.gov/documents/Jefferson/01-31-02-0282.

I have this moment recieved your 2 letters to Mr Randolph & my self (together) and by the same post one from Mr Eppes informing me of the loss of his child. my heart is torn by an event which carries death to hopes so long & fondly cherished by my poor sister. I would give the world to fly to her comfort at this moment but having been dissappointed before in doing what perhaps my *anxiety only* termed a moral duty (visiting her during her lying in) I am afraid to indulge any more hopes upon that subject. to your enquiries relative to poor Jupiter he too has paid the debt to nature; finding himself no better at his return home, he unfortunately conceived him self poisoned & went to consult the negro doctor who attended the George's. he went *in* the house to see uncle Randolph who gave him a dram which he drank & seemed to be as well as he had been for some time past; after which he took a dose from this black doctor who pronounced that it would *kill or cure*. 2½ hours after taking the medecine he fell down in a strong convulsion fit which lasted from ten to elevin hours, during which time it took 3 stout men to hold him, he languished nine days but was never heard to speak from the first of his being seized to the moment of his death. Ursala is I fear going in the same manner with her husband & son, a constant puking shortness or breath and swelling first in the legs but now extending itself the doctor I understand had also given her *means* as they term it and upon Jupiter's death has absconded. I should think his murders sufficiently manifest to come under the cognizance of the law. Mr Trist had left Charlottesville before I recieved your letters but should Mr Randolph be able to procure any other conveyance he will send the peas he is not at home at present I have of course answered those parts of his letter which required an immediate one adieu my dearest Father I have written this with the messenger who is to carry it at my elbow impatiently waiting, I will write by the next post more deliberately we are all well Ellen sends her love to dear *seet* grand papa, believe me with tenderest affection yours

M. Randolph[122]

[122] "To Thomas Jefferson from Martha Jefferson Randolph, 30 January 1800," *Founders Online,* National Archives, last modified June 13, 2018, http://founders.archives.gov/documents/Jefferson/01-31-02-0294.

My dear Martha

I wrote to mr Randolph on the 2d. inst. acknoleging the receipt of his letter of the 18th. Jan. I had one also at the same time from mr Richardson giving me the details from Monticello. the death of Jupiter obliges me to ask of mr. Randolph or yourself to give orders at the proper time in March for the bottling my cyder. I forgot to bring with me a morsel cut from one of our sheets, as a sample to guide mr Barnes in providing some sheeting for me. being entirely ignorant of it myself I must ask the favor of you to inclose me a bit in a letter by the return of post. I suppose our French sheets to be of the proper fineness & quality. a person here has invented the prettiest improvement in the Forte piano I have ever seen. it has tempted me to engage one for Monticello, partly for it's excellence & convenience, partly to assist a very ingenious, modest & poor young man, who ought to make a fortune by his invention. his strings are perpendicular, so that the instrument is only 3. f. 4. I. wide, 16. I. deep, and 3. f. 6. I. high. it resembles when closed the under half of a book case, & may be moved, by it's handles, to the fire side. he contrives within that height to give his strings the same length as in the grand fortepiano, and fixes his 3. unisons to the same screw, which screw is in the direction of the strings and therefore never yields. it scarcely gets out of tune at all, & then for the most part the 3. unisons are tuned at once. the price of one with 5. octaves is 200. D. with 5½ octaves 250. D.

I recieved a letter of Jan. 17. from mr Eppes announcing the death of his child, & that poor Maria was suffering dreadfully, both her breasts having risen & broke. she was still ill from that cause. I have not heard from her since. there is abundant cause of deep concern in this, and especially for the peculiar affliction it will be to them, as I think they would have been made very peculiarly happy by the possession of a child. I am extremely uneasy to hear further from her. the H. of Representatives have sent a resolution to the Senate to adjourn on the 1st. Monday of April. the Eastern men being for the first time eager to get away for political reasons, I think it probable we shall adjourn about that time. there is really no business which ought to keep us one fortnight. I am therefore looking forward with anticipation of the joy of seeing you again ere long, and tasting true happiness in the midst of my family. my absence from you teaches me how essential your society is to my happiness. politics are such a torment that I would advise every one I love not to mix with them. I have changed my circle here according to my wish; abandoning the rich, & declining their dinners & parties, and associating entirely with the class of science, of whom there is a valuable society here. still my wish is to be in the midst of our own families at home. present me affectionately to mr Randolph. kiss all the dear little ones for me. do not let Ellen forget me; and continue to me your love in return for the constant & tenderest attachment of

Your's affectionately

Th: Jefferson[123]

---

[123] "From Thomas Jefferson to Martha Jefferson Randolph, 11 February 1800," *Founders Online,* National Archives, last modified June 13, 2018, http://founders.archives.gov/documents/Jefferson/01-31-02-0311.

Philadelphia Apr. 22. 1800.

My dear Martha

It is very long since I wrote to you, because I have been uncertain whether you would not have left Eppington before the arrival of my letters there, & the rather as I found them very long getting there. mr Randolph's letter of the 12th. informs me you had then returned to Edgehill. in a letter of Mar. 24. which is the last I have recieved from Eppington, mr Eppes informed me Maria was so near well that they expected in a few days to go to Mont-blanco. your departure gives me a hope her cure was at length established. a long & a painful case it has been, & not the most so to herself or those about her. my anxieties have been excessive. I shall go by Mont-blanco to take her home with me, which mr Eppes expressed to be their desire. I wrote last week to mr Richardson to send off my horses to Mont Blanco on the 9th. of May. but both houses having agreed to rise on the 2d Monday (12th. of May) I shall write to him by this post, not to send them off till Friday the 16th. of May; as I shall be 7. or 8 days from the 12th. getting to Mont Blanco, and near a week afterwards getting home. I long once more to get all together again: and still hope, notwithstanding your present establishment, you will pass a great deal of the summer with us. I would wish to urge it just so far as not to break in on your & mr Randolph's desires & convenience. our scenes here can never be pleasant. but they have been less stormy, less painful than during the XYZ. paroxysms. our opponents perceive the decay of their power. still they are pressing it, and trying to pass laws to keep themselves in power. mr Cooper was found guilty two days ago, under the Sedition law, and will be fined & imprisoned. Duane has 16. or 17 suits & indictments against him. the sheriff & justices who got the letters of mr Liston which Sweezy the horse thief abandoned, are indicted. this is all the news I have for mr Randolph. of foreign news we know nothing but what he will see in the papers. I inclose a little story for Anne, and many kisses for Ellen-aroon.

present my affections to mr Randolph. to yourself constant & unbounded love. Adieu my dear dear Martha.[124]

[124] "From Thomas Jefferson to Martha Jefferson Randolph, 22 April 1800," *Founders Online,* National Archives, last modified June 13, 2018, http://founders.archives.gov/documents/Jefferson/01-31-02-0446.

Edgehill May 15 1800

Being prevented by the unexpected arrival of company to day, I have it in my power to write but a few lines to my Dearest Father while the rest of the family sleep. to repeat what he so well knows allready how tenderly loved how anxiously expected he is by every member of the family they are all unwell at present with colds so bad as to create suspicions of the hooping cough particularly the two youngest—Ellen has been very ill we were much disturbed & allarmed for three nights successively being in constant apprehension of her going in to convulsion fits with which she was seriously threatened she is however better tho extremely weak & languid & Anne is quite well for the other two they have constitutions proof against every thing alltho the little one is at the crisis of the disorder what ever it is and has really a horrid cough she has never even been feverish adieu Dear and respected Father hasten I entreat you, the blest moment which will reunite me to all my heart holds dear in the world give my tenderest affections to Maria tell her I would have written to her but for the reason above mentioned not forgetting the dear and amiable family with whom this will find you I remain with an affection truly inexpressible your most tenderly

M. Randolph[125]

[125] "To Thomas Jefferson from Martha Jefferson Randolph, 15 May 1800," *Founders Online*, National Archives, last modified June 13, 2018, http://founders.archives.gov/documents/Jefferson/01-31-02-0486.

My dear Martha

I wrote to mr Randolph on the 9th. & 10th. inst. and yesterday recieved his letter of the 10th. it gave me real joy to learn that Lilly had got a recruit of hands from mr Allen; tho' still I would not have that prevent the taking all from the nailery who are able to cut, as I desired in mine of the 9th. as I wish Craven's ground to be got ready for him without any delay. mr Randolph writes me you are about to wean Cornelia. this must be right & proper. I long to be in the midst of the children, and have more pleasure in their little follies than in the wisdom of the wise. here too there is such a mixture of the bad passions of the heart that one feels themselves in an enemy's country. it is an unpleasant circumstance, if I am destined to stay here, that the great proportion of those of the place who figure, are federalists, and most of them of the violent kind. some have been so personally bitter that they can never forgive me, tho' I do them with sincerity. perhaps in time they will get tamed. our prospect as to the election has been alarming: as a strong disposition exists to prevent an election, & that case not being provided for by the constitution, a dissolution of the government seemed possible. at present there is a prospect that some, tho' federalists, will prefer yielding to the wishes of the people rather than have no government. if I am fixed here, it will be but three easy days journey from you: so that I should hope you & the family could pay an annual visit here at least; which with mine to Monticello of the spring & fall, might enable us to be together 4. or 5. months of the year. on this subject however we may hereafter converse, lest we should be counting chickens before they are hatched. I inclose for Anne a story, too long to be got by heart, but worth reading. kiss them all for me; and keep them in mind of me. tell Ellen I am afraid she has forgotten me. I shall probably be with you the first week in April, as I shall endeavor to be at our court for that month. continue to love me my dear Martha and be assured of my unalterable and tenderest love to you. Adieu.

Th: Jefferson

P.S. Hamilton is using his uttermost influence to procure my election rather than Colo. Burr's.[126]

---

[126] "From Thomas Jefferson to Martha Jefferson Randolph, 16 January 1801," *Founders Online,* National Archives, last modified June 13, 2018, http://founders.archives.gov/documents/Jefferson/01-32-02-0339.

I should not have waited for your letter my Dearest Father had it been in my power to have written sooner but incredible as it may appear, that in period of 2 months not one day could have been found to discharge so sacred and pleasing a duty, it is litterally true that the first fort night of your absence excepted and 3 or 4 days of the last week, I have not been one day capable of attending even to my common domestic affairs. I am again getting into the old way with regard to my stomack, totally unable to digest any thing but a few particular vegetables; harrassed to death by little fevers, for 6 week I scarcely ever missed a night having one untill by recurring to my accustomed remedy in such cases, giving up meat milk coffee and a large proportion of the vegetable tribe that have allways been inimical to my constitution I have at last found some relief. it requires some self denial but I find my self so much recruited both in health and spirits, and every transgression so severely punished, that I shall rigorously adhere to it as long as my health requires it. Cornelia shows the necessity there was for weaning her by her surprising change for the better since that time. the children are all well except Jefferson who cought (that filthiest of all disorders) the itch from a little aprentice boy in the family. he was 6 or seven weeks in constant and familar intercourse with us before we suspected what was the matter with him, the moment it was discovered that the other little boy had it, we were no longer at a loss to account for Jefferson's irruption which had been attributed all along to his covering too warm at night. I am delighted that your return will happen at a season when we shall be able to enjoy your company without interuption. I was at Monticello Last spring 1 day before the arrival of any one, and one day more of interval between the departure of one family and the arrival of another, after which time I never had the pleasure of passing one sociable moment with you. allways in a croud, taken from every useful and

190

pleasing duty to be worried with a multiplicity of disagreable ones which the entertaining of such crouds of company subjects one to in the country, I suffered more in seeing you all ways at a distance than if you had still been in Philadelphia, for then at least I should have enjoyed in anticipation those pleasures which we were deprived of by the concourse of strangers which continually crouded the house when you were with us. I find my self every day becoming more averse to company I have lost my relish for what is usually deemed pleasure, and duties incompatible with it have surplanted all other enjoyments in my breast—the education of my Children to which I have long devoted every moment that I could command, but which is attended with more anxiety now as they increase in age without making those acquirements which other children do. my 2 eldest are uncommonly backward in every thing much more so than many others who have not had half the pains taken with them. Ellen is wonderfully apt. I shall have no trouble with her, but the two others excite serious anxiety with regard to their intellect. of Jefferson my hopes were so little sanguine that I discovered with some surprise & pleasure that he was quicker than I had ever thought it possible for him to be, but he has Lost so much time and will necesarily lose so much more before he can be placed at a good school that I am very unhappy about him. Anne does not want memory but she does not improve. she appears to me to Learn absolutely without profit. adieu my Dear Father we all are painfully anxious to see you. Ellen counts the weeks and continues scoring up complaints against Cornelia whom she is perpetually threatning with *your* displeasure. long is the list of misdemeanors which is to be comunicated to you, amongst which the stealing of 2 potatoes carefully preserved 2 whole days for you but at last Stolen by Cornelia, forms a weighty article. adieu again dearest best beloved Father 2 long months still before we shall see you in the mean time rest assured of the first Place in the heart of your affectionate Child

191

M. Randolph

P.S. by Th:M.R.

Every thing goes on well at Mont'o.—the Nailers all returned to work & executing well some heavy orders, as one from D. Higinb.m for 30.000. Xd. Moses, Jam Hubbard Davy & Shephard still out & to remain till you order otherwise—Joe cuting nails—I had given a charge of lenity respecting all: (Burwell absolutely excepted from the whip alltogether) before you wrote: none have incurred it but the small ones for truancy & yet the work proceeds better than since George. such is the sound sense cleverness & energy of Lillie.[127]

---

[127] "To Thomas Jefferson from Martha Jefferson Randolph and Thomas Mann Randolph, 31 January 1801," *Founders Online,* National Archives, last modified June 13, 2018, http://founders.archives.gov/documents/Jefferson/01-32-02-0375.

My dear Martha

Yours of Jan. 31. is this moment put into my hands, and the departure of the post obliges an answer on the same day. I am much afflicted to learn that your health is not good, and the particular derangement of your stomach. this last is the parent of many ills, and if any degree of abstinence will relieve you from them it ought to be practised. perhaps in time it may be brought to by beginning with a single one of the hostile articles; taking a very little of it at first, & more & more as the stomach habituates itself to it. in this way the catalogue may perhaps be enlarged by article after article. I have formed a different judgment of both Anne & Jefferson from what you do; of Anne positively, of Jefferson possibly. I think her apt, intelligent, good humored & of soft & affectionate dispositions, & that she will make a pleasant, amiable and respectable woman. of Jefferson's dispositions I have formed a good opinion, & have not suffered myself to form any either good or bad of his genius. it is not every heavy-seeming boy which makes a man of judgment, but I never yet saw a man of judgment who had not been a heavy seeming boy, nor knew a boy of what are called sprightly parts become a man of judgment. but I set much less store by talents than good dispositions: and shall be perfectly happy to see Jefferson a good man, industrious farmer, & kind & beloved among all his neighbors: by cultivating these dispositions in him, and they may be immensely strengthened by culture, we may ensure his & our happiness: and genius itself can propose no other object.—nobody can ever have felt so severely as myself the prostration of family society from the circumstance you mention. worn down here with pursuits in which I take no delight, surrounded by enemies & spies catching & perverting every word which falls from my lips or flows from my pen, and inventing where facts fail them, I pant for that society where all is peace and harmony, where we love & are beloved by every object we see. and to have that intercourse of soft affections hushed & suppressed by the eternal presence of strangers goes very hard indeed; & the harder as we see that the candle of life is burning out, so that the pleasures we lose are lost forever. but there is no remedy. the present manners & usages of our country are laws we cannot repeal. they are altering by degrees; & you will live to see the hospitality of the country reduced to the visiting hours of the day, & the family left to tranquility in the evening. it is wise therefore under the necessity of our present situation to view the pleasing side of the medal: and to consider that these visits are evidences of the general esteem which we have been all our lives trying to merit. the character of those we recieve is very different from the loungers who infest the houses of the wealthy in general: nor can it be relieved in our case but by a revolting conduct which would undo the whole labor of our lives. it is a valuable circumstance that it is only thro' a particular portion of the year that these inconveniences arise.—the election by the H. of R. being on Wednesday next, & the next our post day, I shall be able to tell you something certain of it by my next letter. I believe it will be as the people have wished; but this depends on the will of a few moderate men; and they may be controuled by their party. I long to see the time approach when I can be returning to you, tho' it may be for a short time only. these are the only times that existence is of any value to me. continue then to love me my ever dear Martha, and to be assured that to yourself, your sister & those dear to you, every thing in my life is devoted. ambition has no hold on me but thro' you. my personal affections would fix me for ever with you. present me affectionately to mr Randolph. kiss the dear little objects of our mutual love, and be assured of the constancy & tenderness of mine to you. Adieu.

Th: Jefferson[128]

[128] "From Thomas Jefferson to Martha Jefferson Randolph, 5 February 1801," *Founders Online,* National Archives, last modified June 13, 2018, http://founders.archives.gov/documents/Jefferson/01-32-02-0397.

Thomas Jefferson's First Presidential Term

1801 - 1804

Thomas Jefferson would run again for President, but this time he would claim victory. During his time as President he would reside at the President's House.

Patsy would frequently visit him there during his time as President. She would have two more daughters between 1801 through 1804, they were Virginia Jefferson Randolph and Mary Jefferson Randolph.

In 1803, Patsy's husband became a member of Congress.

***

Without further ado,
The letters of Thomas and Patsy,
During Thomas Jefferson's First Term As President

Washington May 28. 1801.

My very dear Martha

 recieved yesterday mr Randolph's letter of the 23d. giving me the always welcome news of your health. I have not heard from Maria since I have been here. it is a terrible thing that people will not write unless they have materials to make a long letter: when three words would be so acceptable. Mrs. Madison left us two days ago, to commence housekeeping, so that Capt Lewis & myself are like two mice in a church. it would be the greatest comfort imaginable to have you or Maria here. but this wish must be subordinate to your family affairs. mrs Madison's stay here enabled me to begin an acquaintance with the ladies of the place, so as to have established the precedent of having them at our dinners. still their future visits will be awkward to themselves in the present construction of our family. I inclose for Anne some trifles cut out of the newspapers. tell Ellen I will send her a pretty story as soon as she can read it. kiss them all for me; my affectionate esteem to mr Randolph & warmest love to yourself.

Th: Jefferson[129]

[129] "From Thomas Jefferson to Martha Jefferson Randolph, 28 May 1801," *Founders Online,* National Archives, last modified June 13, 2018, http://founders.archives.gov/documents/Jefferson/01-34-02-0162.

In an absence of 3 months I blush to think that this is the first time I have
written to my Dear Father. it does not arise however as you suppose from
want of materials, & still less of inclination, but from a spirit of
procrastination which by inducing me to defer allways to the last moment,
finally ocasions the total loss of opportunity. my affection, my thoughts
are however, perpetually with you, incessantly hovering over you, there is
no one scene in your solitary establishment in which they have not visited
you. and never with out deeply regretting the unavoidable necessity of
your spending so much of your time cut off from that society which alone
gives a charm to Life, and which you of all others in the world estimate
most highly. however the time is at hand when every thing will be
forgotten in a blest reunion of every individual of those we most love once
more at Monticello and as the time approaches the spirits of the family
proportionally increase. you have suffered a little from the last tremendous
hail storm, from the circumstance of 2 of the sky lights being uncover'd.
they were totally demolished and I believe it is owing to the accident of
the storm's raging with so much more fury in the valley than on the
mountains that you escaped so much better than your neighbours. the
damage was immense in Charlottesville & Milton, allmost every window
broken in some houses; we also suffered considerably and the more so as
we have not been able to replace in either of the above mentioned places
the glass, which has occasioned us to the violence of every succeeding
rain in a degree that renders the house scarcely tenantable.
your stockings are at last disposed of, but not to my satisfaction because I
am sure they will not be so to yours—Aunt Carr after many ineffectual
efforts to put them *out* acceded at Last to the united and importunate
entreaties of Mrs Randolph & Mrs Lilburn Lewis to Let them knit them
for you; and Aunt Lewis dining with me a few days after and hearing of

the failure of the means upon which I had counted in accomplishing my part of the under taking, insisted in a manner that baffled resistance upon my letting her & her Daughters take them home & do them. it is a disagreable piece of business, but one not to have been fore seen in the first instance and not to be avoided afterwards with out hurting the feelings & perhaps giving offence to those Ladies. inclosed are the samples Fontrice was to have carried, of the cotton one is too fine the other too coarse. a size between the two would answer better than either. the sheeting is also I think rather coarse but not much so. adieu dearest Father, the children are all confusing me with messages of various discriptions but the post hour is past and I am afraid my letter will scarcely be in time. believe me with ardent affection yours

M. Randolph[130]

---

[130] "To Thomas Jefferson from Martha Jefferson Randolph, 19 June 1801," *Founders Online,* National Archives, last modified June 13, 2018, http://founders.archives.gov/documents/Jefferson/01-34-02-0305.

Washington June. 25. 1801.

My dear Martha

Your's of the 19. came to hand yesterday. as it says nothing of your health I presume all are well. I recieved yesterday also a letter from Maria of the 18th. she was then well & preparing to go to Eppington, and in about 4. weeks expected to set out for Albemarle. mr Eppes was engaged in his harvest much obstructed by rain, & regretting he had not before deposited Maria at Monticello. I hope she will get there safe. tho' it is yet more than a month before I can set out for the same destination, yet I begin with pleasure to make memorandums, lay by what is to be carried there &c &c . for the pleasure of thinking of it, of looking forward to the moment when we shall be all there together. amidst the havoc made by the hailstorm in Albemarle I think myself well off to have had only two windows demolished. I should have expected my large panes of glass would have broken easily. I inclose a little story for Anne as I have sometimes done before. tell Ellen as soon as she can read them, I will select some beautiful ones for her. they shall be black, red, yellow, green & of all sorts of colours. I suppose you have had cucumbers & raspberries long ago. neither are yet at market here, tho some private gardens have furnished them. present me affectionately to mr Randolph who I suppose is now busy in his harvest. I rejoice at the prospect of price for wheat, & hope he will be able to take the benefit of the early market. if his own threshing machine is not ready, he is free to send for mine, which is in order & may expedite his getting out. kiss the little ones for me & be assured of my constant & tenderest love.

Th: Jefferson[131]

---

[131] "From Thomas Jefferson to Martha Jefferson Randolph, 25 June 1801," *Founders Online,* National Archives, last modified June 13, 2018, http://founders.archives.gov/documents/Jefferson/01-34-02-0352.

My dear Martha

I recieved yesterday mr Randolph's letter of the 11th. and at the same time one from mr Eppes. he had just carried Maria to Eppington with the loss of a horse on the road. they are to leave Eppington tomorrow at farthest for Monticello, so that by the time you recieve this they will be with you. from what mr Randolph writes I should think you had better go over at once with your sister to Monticello and take up your quarters there. I shall join you in the first seven days of August. in the mean time the inclosed letter to mr Craven (which I pray you to send him) will secure you all the resources for the house which he can supply. Liquors have been sent on & I learn are arrived, tho' with some loss. Lilly has before recieved orders to furnish what he can as if I were there. I wish you would notify him to be collecting geese & ducks and to provide new flour. of lambs I presume he has plenty. I have had groceries waiting here some time for a conveyance. would it not be well for you to send at once for mrs Marks? Remus and my chair are at Monticello, & Phill as usual can go for her. I this day inclose to Dr. Wardlaw some publications on the kine pox, with a request to make himself acquainted with them. I shall probably be able to carry on some infectious matter with a view of trying whether we cannot introduce it there. the first assay here has proved unsuccessful but some matter recieved 6. days ago & immediately used, will prove this day whether it takes or not; & I am promised by Dr. Waterhouse of Boston successive weekly supplies till it takes. if the matter be genuine there is no doubt it prevents the Small pox.—I send you a piece of music sent to me. if the music be no better than the words it will not shine. also some small things for Anne. kiss them all for me. present me affectionately to mr Randolph, & be assured yourself of my warmest love.

Th: Jefferson[132]

[132] "From Thomas Jefferson to Martha Jefferson Randolph, 16 July 1801," *Founders Online,* National Archives, last modified June 13, 2018, http://founders.archives.gov/documents/Jefferson/01-34-02-0441.

Your letters found us all *together* at Edgehill. Maria does not look well but considering all things she seems to be in as good health as can be expected. my own has been uncommonly so, since my return from Monticello. with your request of going over immediately it is utterly impossible to comply; Mrs Bache's family being with us at present, and to remain, untill the Doctor's return. Maria stays with *us* untill you join us and from what she says will not I hope require *my* attentions untill I am *able* to bestow them entirely upon her. we have not sent for Aunt Marks because of the present size of our family which would render it, (with the expected addition) impossible to accomodate her—she might feel hurt at the idea of being alone at Monticello your other commissions shall be faithfully executed with regard to Lilly &c, and altho it will not be in my power to be with you as soon as I could wish yet the idea of being so near you and the pleasure of seeing you sometimes will enliven a time otherwise dreary and monotonous adieu ever dear Father believe me with unchangeable affection yours

M. Randolph[133]

I am in hopes, my dear Martha, that I shall hear by the arrival of tomorrow morning's post, that you are all well. in the mean while the arrangement is such that my letter must go hence this evening. my last letter was from mr Eppes of Oct. 3. when all were well. I inclose a Crazy Jane for Anne, and a sweetheart for Ellen. the latter instead of the many coloured stories which she cannot yet read. from the resolution you had taken I imagine you are now at Edgehill surrounded by the cares and the comforts of your family. I wish they may be less interrupted than at Monticello. I set down this as a year of life lost to myself, having been crouded out of the enjoiment of the family during the only recess I can take in the year. I believe I must hereafter not let it be known when I intend to be at home, & make my visits by stealth. there is real disappointment felt here at neither of you coming with me. I promise them on your faith for the ensuing spring. I wish however that may be found as convenient a season of absence for mr Randolph. mr. Madison & family are with us for a few days, their house having been freshly plaistered & not yet dry enough to go into. such is the drought here that nobody can remember when it rained last. my sincere affections to mr Randolph1 & mr Eppes. kisses to the young ones & my tenderest love to Maria & yourself.

Th: Jefferson[134]

[134] "From Thomas Jefferson to Martha Jefferson Randolph, 19 October 1801," *Founders Online,* National Archives, last modified June 13, 2018, http://founders.archives.gov/documents/Jefferson/01-35-02-0384.

Dearest Father

Mr Trist who will deliver this can also give a better account of the children than (limited as I am for time) I possibly can. however I must write a few lines to you if it is only to wonder at your long silence. each successive post has been anxiously expected and desired, only to bring along with it fresh dissapointment. my sister left us on Monday with her little boy better than could be expected, but in a very precarious state of being. he is (altho healthy except the hooping cough), the most delicate creature I ever beheld. mine are doing well, all but poor Ellen, who looks wretchedly is much reduced and weakened by the cough which still continues upon her with extreme violence. little Virginia is recovering, still distressing us at times but the crisis seems to be over with all of them. it was a terible moment—Ellen and Cornelia were particularly ill both delirious one singing and laughing the other (Ellen) gloomy & terrified equally unconscious of the objects around them. my God what moment for a Parent the agonies of Mr Randolph's mind seemed to call forth every energy of mine I had to act in the double capacity of nurse to my children and comforter to their father. it is of service perhaps to be obliged to exert one self upon those occasions.1 certainly the mind acquires strength by it to bear up against evils that in other circumstances would totally over come it. I am recovering from the fatigue which attended the illness of my children and I am at this moment in more perfect health than I have been for years. adieu beloved Father you would write oftener if you knew how much pleasure your letters give. there is not a child in the house that does not run at the return of the messenger to know if there is a letter from Grand Papa. Stewart your white smith is returned, the plaistering2 at Monticello goes on, not as well as the first room which was elegantly done but better than the 3d & fourth, the two I think you would have been most anxious about, being below stairs. Moran goes on slowly every one the

207

children with the hooping cough excepted is well and they are none of them bad but every thing upon the land (at Monticello) has it. once more adieu. believe me with ardent affection yours

M. Randolph

to tell you it is past one o'clock will appologize for a great deal of incorectness in this scrawl and the hurried way in I generally write will account for the rest—[135]

[135] "To Thomas Jefferson from Martha Jefferson Randolph, 18 November 1801," *Founders Online,* National Archives, last modified June 13, 2018, http://founders.archives.gov/documents/Jefferson/01-35-02-0528.

Washington Nov. 27. 1801.

My dear Martha

Your's of Nov. 18. by mr Trist has been duly recieved. my business is become so intense that when post day comes, it is often out of my power to spare a moment. the post too, being now on the winter establishment is three days longer in carrying our letters. I am sincerely concerned at the situation of our dear little ones with the whooping cough, but much rejoiced that they have past the crisis of the disease safely. there is no disease whatever which I so much dread with children. I have not heard from Maria since she left you: but generally sucking children bear that disease better than those a little past that stage. I hope therefore her little Francis will do well. I am afraid, from what I hear that Moran & Perry have gone on badly with my works at Monticello. I am anxious to see the hull of the buildings once done with. we are all overjoyed with the news of peace. I consider it as the most fortunate thing which could have happened to place the present administration on advantageous ground. the only rock we feared was war; and it did not depend on ourselves but others whether we should keep out of it. we hope Great Britain will have so much to do at home that she will not have time to intrigue and plot against this country. we are now within 10. days of Congress when our campaign will begin & will probably continue to April. I hope I shall continue to hear from you often, and always that the children are doing well. my affections and contemplations are all with you, where indeed all my happiness centers. my cordial esteem to mr Randolph, kisses to the little ones, and tenderest love to yourself.

Th: Jefferson[136]

---

[136] "From Thomas Jefferson to Martha Jefferson Randolph, 27 November 1801," *Founders Online*, National Archives, last modified June 13, 2018, http://founders.archives.gov/documents/Jefferson/01-35-02-0562.

This is merely, my dear Martha, to say that all is well. it is very long since I have heard from you, my last letter from Edgehill being of the 6th. of Dec. a letter of Jan. 6. from mr Eppes at Richmond informed me that Maria was entirely reestablished in her health, & her breast quite well. the little boy too was well & healthy.—Dr. Gantt has inoculated six of his Cow pox patients with the small pox, not one of which took it. many have been tried in Philadelphia, & with the same issue. as the matter here came from Monticello, and that at Philadelphia from this place, they establish the genuineness of our inoculations & may place our families & neighbors in perfect security.   Congress have as yet passed but one bill. the repeal of the Judiciary law is rather doubtful in the Senate, by the absence of two republican Senators. great opposition is made to the reduction of the army, the navy, and the taxes. they will be reduced; but some republican votes will fly the way on the occasion. mr Dawson arrived here three or four days ago. present me affectionately to mr Randolph, and the young ones, and be assured yourself of my constant & tenderest love.

Th: Jefferson

P.S. in my last week's letter to mr Randolph I inclosed one for mr Lilly with 940. D. in it, which I shall be glad to hear got safe to hand.[137]

---

[137] "From Thomas Jefferson to Martha Jefferson Randolph, 17 January 1802," *Founders Online,* National Archives, last modified June 13, 2018, http://founders.archives.gov/documents/Jefferson/01-36-02-0240.

My Dear Martha

recieved Anne's letter by the last post, in which she forgot to mention the health of the family, but I presume it good. I inclose you a medal executed by an artist lately from Europe and who appears to be equal to any in the world. it is taken from Houdon's bust, for he never saw me. it sells the more readily as the prints which have been offered the public are such miserable caracatures. Congress will probably rise within three weeks and I shall be on in a week or ten days afterwards. my last to mr Randolph explained my expectations as to your motions during his journey. I wrote lately to Maria, encouraging her to pay us a flying visit at least while you are here, and proposing to mr Eppes so to time his next plantation visit in Albemarle as to meet me there in the beginning of May. my last information from the Hundred stated them all well, little Francis particularly healthy. Anne writes me that Ellen will be through all her books before I come. she may count therefore on my bringing her a new supply.—I have desired Lilly to make the usual provision of necessaries for me at Monticello, and if he should be at a loss for the particulars to consult with you. my orders as to the garden were to sow & plant as usual, and to furnish you with the proceeds. order them therefore freely: you know they will do nothing if you leave it to their delicacy. I am looking forward with impatience to the moment when I can embrace you in all my affection and the dear children. it already occupies much of my thoughts as the time approaches. present me affectionately to mr Randolph, and be assured yourself of my tenderest love.

Th: Jefferson[138]

---

[138] "From Thomas Jefferson to Martha Jefferson Randolph, 3 April 1802," *Founders Online,* National Archives, last modified June 13, 2018, http://founders.archives.gov/documents/Jefferson/01-37-02-0149.

I recieved with gratitude and pleasure inexpressible, my dearest Father, the elegant medal you sent me. it arrived safely with out a scratch even, and is I think a good likeness; but as I found fault with Houdon for making you too old I shall have the same quarrel with the medal also. you have many years to live before the likeness can be a perfect one. Mr R—desired me to tell you that as his trip to Georgia was but to take a view of the country, a few weeks sooner or later would make no material difference with him and his anxiety to conduct such a family of little children thro the difficulties of the journey would naturally induce him to pospone his as it will be attended by no great inconvenience to himself. Ellen and Cornelia have had an erruption attended with fever which has been prevalent in the neighbourhood certainly not the chicken pox but what else we cannot determine. Ellen is well and Cornelia much better. Virginia is certainly for size and health the finest child I ever had cutting her teeth with out fever, disordered bowels or other indication of her situation but the champing of her gums and the appearance of the teeth them selves. the others go on better than they did last winter. Jefferson is reading latin with his Papa but I am seriously uneasy at his not going to school, Mr Murray with whom we proposed putting him has his number complete and will not I fear take another. Anne translates with tolerable facility, and Ellen reads, not very correctly it is true, but in a way speedily to do so I hope. for which I really think we are indebted to your letter expressing your surprise at her having in so short a time learned to read and write; she began with it her self, and by continually spelling out lines putting them together and then reading them to who ever would listen to her, she convinced me of the practicability of carrying on reading and spelling together before in the regular course of the business she had got into two syllables. the writing she attempted also but the trouble was so much greater than any end to be

answerd by teaching her at so early a period that very reluctantly I
prevailed upon her to defer that part of her education to a more distant
one. so much for my hopes and fears with regard to those objects in which
they center. the former preponderate upon the whole, yet my anxiety about
them frequently makes me unreasonably apprehensive, unreasonably I
think for surely if they turn out well with regard to morals I *ought* to be
satisfied, tho I *feel* that I never can sit down quietly under the idea of their
being blockheads—

adieu Dear adored Father we look forward with transport to the time at
which we shall all meet at monticello tho not on my side unmixed with
pain when I think it will be the precursor of a return to the world from
which I have been so long been secluded and for which my habits render
me every way unfit, tho the pleasure of seeing you every day is a good that
will render every other evil light—once more adieu the children are
clamorous to be remembered to you and believe your self *first* and
unrivaled in the heart of your devoted child

M. Randolph[139]

[139] "To Thomas Jefferson from Martha Jefferson Randolph, 16 April
1802," *Founders Online,* National Archives, last modified June 13, 2018,
http://founders.archives.gov/documents/Jefferson/01-37-02-0208.

My Dear Martha

Your letter of the 16th. and mr Randolph's of the 9th. both came to hand by the last post. since that too I have seen S. Carr who tells me you do not mean to include Virginia and Anne in your visit to this place. against this I must remonstrate. every principal respecting them, and every consideration interesting to yourself, mr Randolph or myself, is in favor of their coming here. if Virginia owes a visit to Dungeoness (as S. Carr says) the winter season will be more safe & convenient for that. knowing that mr Randolph's resources must all be put to the stretch on his visit to Georgia, I insist that they be not touched by any wants which the visit of the family to this place might produce; but that all that shall be mine. as to the article of dress particularly, it can be better furnished here, and I shall intreat that it be so without limitation, as it will not be felt by me. let there be no preparation of that kind therefore but merely to come here. Congress will rise in a few days. I think I can now fix the 5th. or 6th. of May for my departure and the 8th. or 9th. for my being with you. mr & mrs Madison go about the same time: that of their return is unknown to me, but cannot be much later than mine. I think it will be for your ease & convenience to arrive here after mrs Madison's return, and consequently that this will give time for me after I get back here to send a carriage to meet you on a day to be fixed between us. some groceries, intended for use while we are at Monticello, were sent from here a week or 10. days ago. I hope they will arrive in time, and wish their arrival at Milton to be attended to.—mr Milledge will dine with me to-day, and be able perhaps to tell me on what day he will be with you. a mr Clarke, son of Genl. Clarke of Georgia, & a very sensible young man goes with him. I think they will be at Edgehill a day or two after you recieve this. present me affectionately to mr Randolph & the family, & be assured of my tenderest love.

Th: Jefferson

P.S. on further enquiry I doubt if Congress will rise before the last day of the month. this will retard mr Milledge's departure, but not mine.[140]

---

[140] "From Thomas Jefferson to Martha Jefferson Randolph, 24 April 1802," *Founders Online,* National Archives, last modified June 13, 2018, http://founders.archives.gov/documents/Jefferson/01-37-02-0260.

My Dear Martha

I arrived here on Sunday morning (May 30.) to breakfast without having experienced any accident on the road, other than being twice taken in soaking rains: but my water proof coat was a perfect protection. mr and mrs Madison arrived the day after. I find they have not yet got clear of the measles here, so that either at home or here your family will hardly escape it. it is now time for you to fix a day for my having you met at mr Strode's, and it would be well if you could do it so that a postday should intervene, & give me an opportunity of acknoleging the reciept of your letter so that you may be sure it has not miscarried. observe that the post which leaves Milton on Monday cannot carry back an answer till the Sunday following, & that which leaves Milton on Friday, returns with an answer on the Thursday following, taking a compleat week each. I will state on the 2d. leaf of this letter the stages and distances of the road & some notes. you must let me know whether you would rather that I should send horses & a carriage, or horses alone, as it will be perfectly equal to the person who furnishes me. I shall send John with them as the driver will not be acquainted with the road, and it is a difficult one to find. it is generally a good & a safe one except the last day's journey which is very hilly, and will require you to get out of the carriage in several places on the Alexandria road between Fairfax court house & Colo. Wren's which is 8. miles, and once after you pass Wren's. I am not without fear that the measles may have got into your family, and delay the pleasure of seeing you here: but I expect to hear from you by the post which arrives tomorrow morning. my affectionate attachment to mr Randolph, kisses to the children, and tenderest love to yourself.

Th: Jefferson[141]

---

[141] "From Thomas Jefferson to Martha Jefferson Randolph, 3 June 1802," *Founders Online,* National Archives, last modified June 13, 2018, http://founders.archives.gov/documents/Jefferson/01-37-02-0432-0001.

I recieved, my dear daughter, your's of the 13th. by post. I regret
extremely the situation of your family, not only for my disappointment
here, but for what they are to suffer. I acknolege that, knowing when I
came away the measles were in the neighborhood, I saw it was but too
possible your visit here would be delayed. as it is, we must agree to the
fall visit, and as Maria will be at Monticello, I trust she will come on with
you. I believe we shall conclude here to leave this place the last week of
July; probably I shall be with you by the 24th. say 5. weeks from this time,
and I shall endeavor that mr Eppes & Maria be there also by that time. I
hope Peter Hemings will get the better of his complaint, or I know not
what we should do, as it is next to impossible to send Ursula & her child
home & bring them back again.—the servants here have felt great
disappointment at your not coming. the coachman is particularly
chagrined. I suppose he wishes to have an opportunity of shewing himself
on his box; which with me he has never had. mr and mrs Trist are to set
out in a very few days for Albemarle, and I believe the two young ladies
go with them. he, I fancy will proceed immediately to the Missisipi.—
present my best esteem to mr Randolph, abundance of soft things to the
children, and warmest affections to yourself.

Th: Jefferson[142]

---

[142] "From Thomas Jefferson to Martha Jefferson Randolph, 18 June
1802," *Founders Online,* National Archives, last modified June 13, 2018,
http://founders.archives.gov/documents/Jefferson/01-37-02-0509.

Washington July 2. 1802.

My dear Martha

  yesterday recieved letters from mr Eppes & Maria. she has been for a considerable time very unwell, with low but constant fevers, and the child very unwell also. mrs Eppes had gone there and staid with her till she was well enough to be removed to Eppington, where the air & the bark had already produced a favorable effect. she wishes to proceed to Monticello as soon as she is strong enough, but is in dreadful apprehensions from the measles. not having heard from you she was uninformed whether it was in your family. I have this day informed her it is there, and advised her when she goes, to pass directly on to Monticello; and that I would ask the favor of mr Randolph & yourself to take measures for having the mountain clear of it by the 15th. of this month, by which time she may possibly arrive there, or by the 20th. at farthest. after that date should any one on the mountain have it they must remove. Squire's house would be a good place for the nail boys, should they have it, and Betty Hemings's for Bet's or Sally's children. there are no other children on the mountain. I shall be at home from the 25th. to the 28th. my affectionate esteem to mr Randolph and tenderest love to yourself.

Th: Jefferson[143]

[143] "From Thomas Jefferson to Martha Jefferson Randolph, 2 July 1802," *Founders Online,* National Archives, last modified June 13, 2018, http://founders.archives.gov/documents/Jefferson/01-38-02-0013.

My children have escaped the measles most wonderfully and unaccountably for so strongly were we all prepossessed with the idea of it's being impossible that from the moment of it's appearing upon the plantation I rather courted than avoided the infection and the children have been on a regimen for 4 or 5 weeks in the constant expectation of breaking out. Ann has been twice declared full of it once by Doctor Bache and another time by the whole family but it went in as sudenly as it came out and has left much uneasiness upon my mynd for fear of her being subject to something like Mrs Kingkade's I think the smoothness of her skin is affected by it and it shews, upon her heating herself immediately. Cornelia has been very low The sickness which I mentioned to you in my last was but the beginning of a very long and teasing complaint of which however she is getting the better she is still very pale and much emaciated but has recovered her appetite and spirits and I hope will be perfectly well before you return we are entirely free from the measles here now those of our people who had it have recovered and Mr Walton's family living on the same plantation every individual of which had it are all recovered the intercourse between them and us thro the servants was daily yet it has stopped and there is not at this moment one instance of it here. at Monticello the last time I heard from there 3 of the nail boys had it and other's were complaining but whether with the measles or not I could not learn I will send over to Lilly immediately to let him know your orders upon the subject I regret extremely my children having missed it the season was so favorable and it was so mild generally that no time or circumstance for the future can ever be as favorable again, besides having had the anxiety for nothing. I delayed writing to Maria untill I could give her a favorable account, for I know she has had great apprehensions on that score for a long time past adieu my dear Papa I do not know if I gave you a list of the things most wanting in the house I do not exactly recollect what they were but sheets, towels counterpanes and tea china were I think foremost on the list your linen has not arrived or it would have been made up before your return the children all join in love and anxious prayer that nothing may retard your wished for return and believe me with tenderest affections yours

M Randolph

Peter Hemmings is entirely well[144]

---

[144] "To Thomas Jefferson from Martha Jefferson Randolph, 10 July 1802," *Founders Online,* National Archives, last modified June 13, 2018, http://founders.archives.gov/documents/Jefferson/01-38-02-0047.

My Dear Martha

I arrived here on the fourth day of our journey without accident. travelling early one or two mornings through fog brought on some degree of indisposition, which I felt strongly on the day & day after my arrival, but it is wearing off slowly. it has been chiefly an excessive soreness all over and a deafness & ringing in the head. I have desired mr Jefferson to procure you whatever you may call for on my account, and I pray you to do it freely. it never was my intention that a journey made for my gratification should bring any expence on you. I must press on you to let me send horses to meet you, as I am convinced that no horses after the three first days journey, can encounter the 4th. which is hilly beyond any thing you have ever seen below the mountains. I shall expect soon to hear from you. present me affectionately to mr Randolph & kiss the children for me. to yourself my tenderest love.

Th: Jefferson[145]

---

[145] "From Thomas Jefferson to Martha Jefferson Randolph, 7 October 1802," *Founders Online,* National Archives, last modified June 13, 2018, http://founders.archives.gov/documents/Jefferson/01-38-02-0420.

My Dear Martha

have been expecting by every post to learn from you when I might send
on to meet you. I still expect it daily. in the mean time I inclose you 100.
Dol. for the expences of yourself, Maria & all your party. mr Randolph
would do well to exchange the bills for gold & silver which will be more
readily on the road. the indisposition I mentioned in my letter by Bowles
turned out to be rheumatic. it confined me to the house some days, but is
now nearly gone off so that I ride out daily. the hour of the post obliges me
to conclude here with my affectionate attachment to mr Randolph &
tender love to yourself & the children.

Th: Jefferson[146]

[146] "From Thomas Jefferson to Martha Jefferson Randolph, 18 October 1802," *Founders Online,* National Archives, last modified June 13, 2018, http://founders.archives.gov/documents/Jefferson/01-38-02-0482.

October 29

Dear Papa

We recieved your letter and are preparing with all speed to obey its summons, by next friday I hope we shall be able to fix a day, and probably the shortest time in which the horses can be sent after recieving our letter will determine it. tho as yet it is not entirely certain that we can get off so soon. will you be so good as to send orders to the milliner Mde Pick I believe her name is, thro Mrs Madison who very obligingly offered to execute any little commission for us, to send to Philadelphia for 2 wigs of the colour of the hair enclosed and of the most fashionable shapes, that they may be at Washington when we arrive they are universally worn and will relieve us as to the necessity of dressing our own hair a business in which neither of us are adepts I believe Mde. Pick is in the habit of doing those things when desired and they can be procured in a short time from Philadelphia where she corresponds much handsomer and cheaper than elsewhere. adieu Dearest Father Maria is with in good health and Spirits believe me with tender affection

yours

M. Randolph[147]

[147] "To Thomas Jefferson from Martha Jefferson Randolph, 29 October 1802," *Founders Online,* National Archives, last modified June 13, 2018, http://founders.archives.gov/documents/Jefferson/01-38-02-0537.

Washington Nov. 2. 1802.

My Dear Martha

Your letter of the 29th. has relieved me from the great anxiety I had felt on your previous entire silence about your journey. there was no hair inclosed in your letter: but I sent the letter to mrs Madison who has had the order given as you desired, for colours from her own judgment, perhaps those of your own hair. if this should not please, send hair in your Friday's letter, and within a fortnight from that time others suitable can be here from Philadelphia. remember to tell me in your next whether I am to send a carriage, or whether you prefer coming on in your own. it makes no odds here whether horses are sent with or without a carriage.—I spoke to you soon after the arrival of my sister Marks about getting necessaries for her from Higginbotham's. it escaped me to repeat it when I came away. I hope however it has been done, or that she may be still with you & it can yet be done.—pray enable yourself to direct us here how to make muffins in Peter's method. my cook here cannot succeed at all in them, and they are a great luxury to me. deliver to my dear Maria my love, & my rebukes that she should not once have written to me. kiss the little ones, and be assured yourself of my unceasing affections.

Th: Jefferson[148]

Dear Papa

It will be more convenient to us to leave this on wednesday than monday it will occasion a delay of 2 days only, as this is a flying visit only to shew that we are in earnest with regard to Washington I have determined to leave the children all but Jefferson considering the lateness of the season and the bad weather we may reasonably expect in december. The short time shall have to spend with you it is better to part with them for a time than risk such a journey with a carriage full of small children. next spring I hope I shall have it in my power to return with you and carry them all. Maria thinks it would be better to send a carriage with the horses as Mr. Eppes' in which we shall go is much out of repair and ours absolutely not in a travelling condition. adieu Dearest Father yours most truly affectionate

M R[149]

---

[149] "To Thomas Jefferson from Martha Jefferson Randolph, 9 November 1802," *Founders Online,* National Archives, last modified June 13, 2018, http://founders.archives.gov/documents/Jefferson/01-38-02-0584.

My dear Martha

The last post-days have slipt away from me without adverting to them till too late. I learnt by a letter from Maria that you all got home safe, after a very disagreeable journey. indeed I suffered for you in imagination beyond any thing I had long felt. I found the road, in the short distance I went with you, so much worse than I expected, that I augured a dreadful journey, and sincerely lamented you did not await a better time. I felt my solitude too after your departure very severely.—your acquaintances here are well, except mrs Brent & mrs Burrowes. I find mr Lilly was to begin filling his icehouse the 21st. we have had no thaw here since that till yesterday, & the river is still entirely blocked up; so that if the weather has corresponded there, I am in hopes he will have got his house full. I must pray you to press on the making my shirts, so that I may have them on my arrival, which will probably be the 9th. of March. Edy has a son, & is doing well. —I inclose poetry for Anne's book. I must pray her to become my correspondent. it will be useful to her, and very satisfactory to me. Jefferson promised to write to me from Orange court house but was not as good as his word. I presume you were amused with the reciepts for making panne-quaiques and other good things. present my affectionate respects to mr Randolph, kisses to the young ones, and be assured of my tenderest love to yourself.

Th: Jefferson[150]

---

[150] "From Thomas Jefferson to Martha Jefferson Randolph, 27 January 1803," *Founders Online,* National Archives, last modified June 13, 2018, http://founders.archives.gov/documents/Jefferson/01-39-02-0349.

My dear Martha

A promise made to a friend some years ago, but executed only lately, has placed my religious creed on paper. I have thought it just that my family, by possessing this, should be enabled to estimate the libels published against me on this, as on every other possible subject. I have written to Philadelphia for Doctr. Priestley's history of the corruptions of Christianity, which I will send you, & recommend to an attentive perusal, because it establishes the groundwork of my view of this subject.

I have not had a line from Monticello or Edgehill since I parted with you. P. Carr, & mrs Carr, who staid with me 5. or 6. days, told me Cornelia had got happily through her measles, & that Ellen had not taken them. but what has become of Anne? I thought I had her promise to write once a week, at least the words 'all's well.'   It is now time for you to let me know when you expect to be able to set out for Washington, and whether your own carriage can bring you half way. I think my Chickasaws, if drove moderately, will bring you well that far. mr Lilly knows you will want them, & can add a fourth. I think that by changing horses half way, you will come with more comfort. I have no gentleman to send for your escort. finding here a beautiful blue Casimir, waterproof, and thinking it will be particularly à propòs for mr Randolph as a travelling coat for his journey, I have taken enough for that purpose, and will send it to mr Benson, postmaster at Fredericksbg to be forwarded by Abrahams, & hope it will be recieved in time.   mr & mrs Madison will set out for Orange about the last day of the month. they will stay there but a week.—I write to Maria to-day, but supposing her at the Hundred, according to what she told me of her movements, I send my letter there.—I wish you to come on as early as possible: because tho' the members of the government remain here to the last week in July, yet the sickly season commences in fact by the middle of that month: and it would not be safe for you to keep the children here longer than that, lest any one of them being taken sick early, might detain the whole here till the season of general danger, & perhaps through it. kiss the children for me. present me affectionately to mr Randolph, & accept yourself assurances of my constant & tenderest love.

Th: Jefferson[151]

---

[151] "From Thomas Jefferson to Martha Jefferson Randolph, 25 April 1803," *Founders Online,* National Archives, last modified June 13, 2018, http://founders.archives.gov/documents/Jefferson/01-40-02-0198.

So constant, my dear daughter, have been my occupations here since Congress met, that it has never been in my power to write any thing which could admit of delay at all: and our post now passing but once a week, lessens the opportunities, tho the rapidity is increased to 24. hours between this place & Charlottesville. I recieved by mr Randolph the frills & a pair of stockings. it will be impossible to judge as to the proportion of fur until the season comes for wearing them. I think that with the stock I now have, a supply of 2. pair every winter will keep me furnished. I judge from your letter that you are approaching an interesting term, & consequently we shall be anxious to hear from you or of you by every post. I hope you have mrs Suddarth with you, & that on the first alarm you will require the attendance of a physician, because being on the spot, a word of advice often saves a case from being serious which a little delay would render so. never fail therefore to use this precaution. we are all well here, but immersed in the usual bickerings of a political campaign. the feds are few, with little talent on their side, but as much gall at least as those who are wicked & impotent usually have. how much happier you in the midst of your family, with no body approaching you but in love and good will. it is a most desireable situation, & in exchanging it for the scenes of this place we certainly do not calculate well for our happiness. Jerome Bonaparte is to be married tomorrow to a miss Patterson of Baltimore.—give my warm affections to my Maria & tell her my next letter shall be to her. kiss all the fireside, and be assured yourself of my never-ceasing love.

Th: Jefferson[152]

[152] "From Thomas Jefferson to Martha Jefferson Randolph, 7 November 1803," *Founders Online,* National Archives, last modified June 13, 2018, http://founders.archives.gov/documents/Jefferson/01-41-02-0507.

Washington Jan. 23. 04.

My dear Martha

Our Milton post not having come in last night, we are without news from you. I suppose he has been delayed by the weather, a severe snow storm having begun yesterday morning & still continuing. the snow is supposed to be now a foot deep, and is still falling with unabated fury. as it is the first, so I hope it will be the last of our severe winter weather. it is so tempestuous that I presume Congress will hardly meet to-day; & the rather as they have nothing pressing. the little before them will permit them to proceed at leisure, and finish when they please, which I conjecture will be about the 2d. week of March. I expect that mr Eppes will leave it before it rises in order to be with Maria at the knock of the elbow in February. I hope she will keep up her spirits. should she be later than she has calculated, perhaps we may all be with her. altho' the recurrence of those violent attacks to which Francis is liable, cannot but give uneasiness as to their character, yet be that what it will, there is little doubt but he will out-grow them; as I have scarcely ever known an instance to the contrary, at his age.—On Friday Congress give a dinner on the acquisition of Louisiana. they determine to invite no foreign ministers, to avoid questions of etiquette, in which we are enveloped by Merry's & Yrujo's families. as much as I wished to have had yourself & sister with me, I rejoice you were not here. the brunt of the battle now falls on the Secretary's ladies, who are dragged in the dirt of every federal paper. you would have been the victims had you been here, and butchered the more bloodily as they would hope it would be more felt by myself. it is likely to end in those two families putting themselves into Coventry until they recieve orders from their courts to acquiesce in our principles of the equality of all persons meeting together in society, & not to expect to force us into their principles of allotment into ranks & orders. pour into the bosom of my dear Maria all the comfort & courage which the affections of

231

my heart can give her, and tell her to rise superior to all fear, for all our sakes. kiss all the little ones for me, with whom I should be so much happier than here; and be assured yourself of my tender & constant love.

Th: Jefferson[15]

[153] "From Thomas Jefferson to Martha Jefferson Randolph, 23 January 1804," *Founders Online,* National Archives, last modified June 13, 2018, http://founders.archives.gov/documents/Jefferson/01-42-02-0290.

Your letter of the 2d. my dear Martha, which was not recieved till the last night has raised me to life again. for four days past I had gone through inexpressible anxiety. the mail which left you on the 5th. will probably be here tonight, and will I hope strengthen our hopes of Maria's continuing to recover, and mr Eppes's arrival which I presume was on the 6th. will render her spirits triumphant over her Physical debility. Congress have determined to rise on Monday sennight (the 19th.) mr Randolph will probably be with you on the 22d. and myself within 3. or 4. days after. Maria must in the mean time resolve to get strong to make us all happy. your apologies my dear for using any thing at Monticello for her, yourself, family or friends, are more than unnecessary. what is there is as much for the use of you all as for myself, and you cannot do me greater pleasure than by using every thing with the same freedom I should do myself. tell my dear Maria to be of good chear, and to be ready to mount on horseback with us and continue to let us hear of her by every post. if mrs Lewis be still with you deliver her my affectionate respects and assurances of my great sensibility for her kind attentions to Maria. kiss the little ones for me, and be assured of my tenderest love to Maria & yourself.

Th: Jefferson[154]

---

[154] "From Thomas Jefferson to Martha Jefferson Randolph, 8 March 1804," *Founders Online,* National Archives, last modified June 13, 2018, http://founders.archives.gov/documents/Jefferson/01-42-02-0532.

Author's Note

I believe Thomas Jefferson is perhaps one of the most important figures in American History. Through reading his letters we can gain a better understanding of who he was as a person.

There is no doubt the love between Thomas and his daughter. Reading their letters give us insight which we may have originally overlooked.

Personally, Thomas Jefferson is my favorite of the Founding Fathers, and I greatly enjoy his work. It was a thrill compiling this collection.

Acknowledgments

Fist off I would like to thank Thomas Jefferson and Martha Jefferson Randolph. I would also like to thank my parents for installing a love of history in me. I would also like to thank my friends who discuss history with me and keep the conversation interesting. Finally, I would like to thank you the reader.

Bibliography

[1] [3] [5] Thomas Jefferson. (n.d.). Retrieved from https://www.whitehouse.gov/about-the-white-house/presidents/thomas-jefferson/?utm_source=link

[2] [4] Thomas Jefferson Biography. (n.d.). Retrieved from https://www.nps.gov/jeff/learn/historyculture/thomas-jefferson-biography.htm

[6] "From Thomas Jefferson to Martha Jefferson, 28 November 1783," *Founders Online,* National Archives, last modified June 13, 2018, http://founders.archives.gov/documents/Jefferson/01-06-02-0286.

[7] "From Thomas Jefferson to Martha Jefferson, 11 December 1783," *Founders Online,* National Archives, last modified June 13, 2018, http://founders.archives.gov/documents/Jefferson/01-06-02-0303.

[8] "From Thomas Jefferson to Martha Jefferson, 22 December 1783," *Founders Online,* National Archives, last modified June 13, 2018, http://founders.archives.gov/documents/Jefferson/01-06-02-0322.

[9] "From Thomas Jefferson to Martha Jefferson, 15 January 1784," *Founders Online,* National Archives, last modified June 13, 2018, http://founders.archives.gov/documents/Jefferson/01-06-02-0358.

[10] "From Thomas Jefferson to Martha Jefferson, 18 February 1784," *Founders Online,* National Archives, last modified June 13, 2018, http://founders.archives.gov/documents/Jefferson/01-06-02-0404.

[11] "From Thomas Jefferson to Martha Jefferson, 19 March 1784," *Founders Online,* National Archives, last modified June 13, 2018, http://founders.archives.gov/documents/Jefferson/01-07-02-0041.

[12] "From Thomas Jefferson to Martha Jefferson, 4 April 1784," *Founders Online,* National Archives, last modified June 13, 2018, http://founders.archives.gov/documents/Jefferson/01-07-02-0069.

[13] "From Thomas Jefferson to Martha Jefferson, 17 April 1784," *Founders Online,* National Archives, last modified June 13, 2018, http://founders.archives.gov/documents/Jefferson/01-07-02-0104.

[14] "From Thomas Jefferson to Martha Jefferson, 6 March 1786," *Founders Online,* National Archives, last modified June 13, 2018, http://founders.archives.gov/documents/Jefferson/01-09-02-0286.

[15] "To Thomas Jefferson from Martha Jefferson, 8 [March] 1787," *Founders Online,* National Archives, last modified June 13, 2018, http://founders.archives.gov/documents/Jefferson/01-11-02-0215.

[16] "To Thomas Jefferson from Martha Jefferson, 8 [March] 1787," *Founders Online,* National Archives, last modified June 13, 2018, http://founders.archives.gov/documents/Jefferson/01-11-02-0215.

[17] "From Thomas Jefferson to Martha Jefferson, 28 March 1787," *Founders Online,* National Archives, last modified June 13, 2018, http://founders.archives.gov/documents/Jefferson/01-11-02-0244.

[18] "From Thomas Jefferson to Martha Jefferson, 7 April 1787," *Founders Online,* National Archives, last modified June 13, 2018, http://founders.archives.gov/documents/Jefferson/01-11-02-0266.

[19] "To Thomas Jefferson from Martha Jefferson, 9 April 1787," *Founders Online,* National Archives, last modified June 13, 2018, http://founders.archives.gov/documents/Jefferson/01-11-02-0270.

[20] "To Thomas Jefferson from Martha Jefferson, 3 May 1787," *Founders Online,* National Archives, last modified June 13, 2018, http://founders.archives.gov/documents/Jefferson/01-11-02-0316.

[21] "From Thomas Jefferson to Martha Jefferson, 5 May 1787," *Founders Online,* National Archives, last modified June 13, 2018, http://founders.archives.gov/documents/Jefferson/01-11-02-0327.

[22] "From Thomas Jefferson to Martha Jefferson, 21 May 1787," *Founders Online,* National Archives, last modified June 13, 2018, http://founders.archives.gov/documents/Jefferson/01-11-02-0350.

[23] "To Thomas Jefferson from Martha Jefferson, 27 May 1787," *Founders Online,* National Archives, last modified June 13, 2018, http://founders.archives.gov/documents/Jefferson/01-11-02-0366.

[24] "From Thomas Jefferson to Martha Jefferson, 1 June 1787," *Founders Online,* National Archives, last modified June 13, 2018, http://founders.archives.gov/documents/Jefferson/01-11-02-0374.

[25] "From Thomas Jefferson to Martha Jefferson, 14 June 1787," *Founders Online,* National Archives, last modified June 13, 2018, http://founders.archives.gov/documents/Jefferson/01-11-02-0400.

[26] "From Thomas Jefferson to Martha Jefferson, 6 July [1787]," *Founders Online,* National Archives, last modified June 13, 2018, http://founders.archives.gov/documents/Jefferson/01-15-02-0616.

[27] "From Thomas Jefferson to Martha Jefferson, 16 June 1788," *Founders Online,* National Archives, last modified June 13, 2018, http://founders.archives.gov/documents/Jefferson/01-27-02-0703.

[28] "From Thomas Jefferson to Martha Jefferson Randolph, 4 April 1790," *Founders Online,* National Archives, last modified June 13, 2018, http://founders.archives.gov/documents/Jefferson/01-16-02-0172.

[29] "To Thomas Jefferson from Martha Jefferson Randolph, 25 April 1790," *Founders Online,* National Archives, last modified June 13, 2018, http://founders.archives.gov/documents/Jefferson/01-16-02-0218.

[30] "From Thomas Jefferson to Martha Jefferson Randolph, 26 April 1790," *Founders Online,* National Archives, last modified June 13, 2018, http://founders.archives.gov/documents/Jefferson/01-16-02-0220.

[31] "From Thomas Jefferson to Martha Jefferson Randolph, 16 May 1790," *Founders Online,* National Archives, last modified June 13, 2018, http://founders.archives.gov/documents/Jefferson/01-16-02-0250.

[32] "From Thomas Jefferson to Martha Jefferson Randolph, 6 June 1790," *Founders Online,* National Archives, last modified June 13, 2018, http://founders.archives.gov/documents/Jefferson/01-16-02-0272.

[33] "From Thomas Jefferson to Martha Jefferson Randolph, 27 June 1790," *Founders Online,* National Archives, last modified June 13, 2018, http://founders.archives.gov/documents/Jefferson/01-16-02-0340.

[34] "From Thomas Jefferson to Martha Jefferson Randolph, 17 July 1790," *Founders Online,* National Archives, last modified June 13, 2018, http://founders.archives.gov/documents/Jefferson/01-17-02-0023.

[35] "From Thomas Jefferson to Martha Jefferson Randolph, 8 August 1790," *Founders Online,* National Archives, last modified June 13, 2018, http://founders.archives.gov/documents/Jefferson/01-17-02-0084.

[36] "From Thomas Jefferson to Martha Jefferson Randolph, 22 August 1790," *Founders Online,* National Archives, last modified June 13, 2018, http://founders.archives.gov/documents/Jefferson/01-17-02-0111.

[37] "From Thomas Jefferson to Martha Jefferson Randolph, 1 December 1790," *Founders Online,* National Archives, last modified June 13, 2018, http://founders.archives.gov/documents/Jefferson/01-18-02-0078.

[38] "From Thomas Jefferson to Martha Jefferson Randolph, 23 December 1790," *Founders Online,* National Archives, last modified June 13, 2018, http://founders.archives.gov/documents/Jefferson/01-18-02-0127.

[39] "To Thomas Jefferson from Martha Jefferson Randolph, 16 January 1791," *Founders Online,* National Archives, last modified June 13, 2018, http://founders.archives.gov/documents/Jefferson/01-18-02-0173.

[40] "From Thomas Jefferson to Martha Jefferson Randolph, 20 January 1791," *Founders Online,* National Archives, last modified June 13, 2018, http://founders.archives.gov/documents/Jefferson/01-18-02-0187.

[41] "From Thomas Jefferson to Martha Jefferson Randolph, 2 February 1791," *Founders Online,* National Archives, last modified June 13, 2018, http://founders.archives.gov/documents/Jefferson/01-19-02-0017.

[42] "From Thomas Jefferson to Martha Jefferson Randolph, 9 February 1791," *Founders Online,* National Archives, last modified June 13, 2018, http://founders.archives.gov/documents/Jefferson/01-19-02-0039.

[43] "From Thomas Jefferson to Martha Jefferson Randolph, 2 March 1791," *Founders Online,* National Archives, last modified June 13, 2018, http://founders.archives.gov/documents/Jefferson/01-19-02-0096.

[44] "To Thomas Jefferson from Martha Jefferson Randolph, 22 March 1791," *Founders Online,* National Archives, last modified June 13, 2018, http://founders.archives.gov/documents/Jefferson/01-19-02-0160.

[45] "From Thomas Jefferson to Martha Jefferson Randolph, 24 March 1791," *Founders Online,* National Archives, last modified June 13, 2018, http://founders.archives.gov/documents/Jefferson/01-19-02-0165.

[46] "From Thomas Jefferson to Martha Jefferson Randolph, 17 April 1791," *Founders Online,* National Archives, last modified June 13, 2018, http://founders.archives.gov/documents/Jefferson/01-20-02-0052.

[47] "To Thomas Jefferson from Martha Jefferson Randolph, 23 May 1791," *Founders Online,* National Archives, last modified June 13, 2018, http://founders.archives.gov/documents/Jefferson/01-20-02-0177.

[48] "V. Thomas Jefferson to Martha Jefferson Randolph, 31 May 1791," *Founders Online,* National Archives, last modified June 13, 2018, http://founders.archives.gov/documents/Jefferson/01-20-02-0173-0006.

[49] "From Thomas Jefferson to Martha Jefferson Randolph, 23 June 1791," *Founders Online,* National Archives, last modified June 13, 2018, http://founders.archives.gov/documents/Jefferson/01-20-02-0217.

[50] "From Thomas Jefferson to Martha Jefferson Randolph, 10 July 1791," *Founders Online,* National Archives, last modified June 13, 2018, http://founders.archives.gov/documents/Jefferson/01-20-02-0268.

[51] "From Thomas Jefferson to Martha Jefferson Randolph, 24 July 1791," *Founders Online,* National Archives, last modified June 13, 2018, http://founders.archives.gov/documents/Jefferson/01-20-02-0319.

[52] "From Thomas Jefferson to Martha Jefferson Randolph, 14 August 1791," *Founders Online,* National Archives, last modified June 13, 2018, http://founders.archives.gov/documents/Jefferson/01-22-02-0041.

[53] "From Thomas Jefferson to Martha Jefferson Randolph, 13 November 1791," *Founders Online,* National Archives, last modified June 13, 2018, http://founders.archives.gov/documents/Jefferson/01-22-02-0270.

[54] "From Thomas Jefferson to Martha Jefferson Randolph, 4 December 1791," *Founders Online,* National Archives, last modified June 13, 2018, http://founders.archives.gov/documents/Jefferson/01-22-02-0340.

[55] "From Thomas Jefferson to Martha Jefferson Randolph, 25 December 1791," *Founders Online,* National Archives, last modified June 13, 2018, http://founders.archives.gov/documents/Jefferson/01-22-02-0419.

[56] "From Thomas Jefferson to Martha Jefferson Randolph, 15 January 1792," *Founders Online,* National Archives, last modified June 13, 2018, http://founders.archives.gov/documents/Jefferson/01-23-02-0043.

[57] "From Thomas Jefferson to Martha Jefferson Randolph, 5 February 1792," *Founders Online,* National Archives, last modified June 13, 2018, http://founders.archives.gov/documents/Jefferson/01-23-02-0101.

[58] "To Thomas Jefferson from Martha Jefferson Randolph, 20 February 1792," *Founders Online,* National Archives, last modified June 13, 2018, http://founders.archives.gov/documents/Jefferson/01-23-02-0126.

[59] "From Thomas Jefferson to Martha Jefferson Randolph, 26 February 1792," *Founders Online,* National Archives, last modified June 13, 2018, http://founders.archives.gov/documents/Jefferson/01-23-02-0149.

[60] "From Thomas Jefferson to Martha Jefferson Randolph, 22 March 1792," *Founders Online,* National Archives, last modified June 13, 2018, http://founders.archives.gov/documents/Jefferson/01-23-02-0272.

[61] "From Thomas Jefferson to Martha Jefferson Randolph, 6 April 1792," *Founders Online,* National Archives, last modified June 13, 2018, http://founders.archives.gov/documents/Jefferson/01-23-02-0333.

[62] "From Thomas Jefferson to Martha Jefferson Randolph, 27 April 1792," *Founders Online,* National Archives, last modified June 13, 2018, http://founders.archives.gov/documents/Jefferson/01-23-02-0418.

[63] "To Thomas Jefferson from Martha Jefferson Randolph, 7 May 1792," *Founders Online,* National Archives, last modified June 13, 2018, http://founders.archives.gov/documents/Jefferson/01-23-02-0442.

[64] "From Thomas Jefferson to Martha Jefferson Randolph, 11 May 1792," *Founders Online,* National Archives, last modified June 13, 2018, http://founders.archives.gov/documents/Jefferson/01-23-02-0453.

[65] "From Thomas Jefferson to Martha Jefferson Randolph, 27 May 1792," *Founders Online,* National Archives, last modified June 13, 2018, http://founders.archives.gov/documents/Jefferson/01-23-02-0499.

[66] "To Thomas Jefferson from Martha Jefferson Randolph, 27 May 1792," *Founders Online,* National Archives, last modified June 13, 2018, http://founders.archives.gov/documents/Jefferson/01-23-02-0500.

[67] "From Thomas Jefferson to Martha Jefferson Randolph, 8 June 1792," *Founders Online,* National Archives, last modified June 13, 2018, http://founders.archives.gov/documents/Jefferson/01-24-02-0039.

[68] "From Thomas Jefferson to Martha Jefferson Randolph, 22 June 1792," *Founders Online,* National Archives, last modified June 13, 2018, http://founders.archives.gov/documents/Jefferson/01-24-02-0108.

[69] "To Thomas Jefferson from Martha Jefferson Randolph, 2 July 1792," *Founders Online,* National Archives, last modified June 13, 2018, http://founders.archives.gov/documents/Jefferson/01-24-02-0151.

[70] "From Thomas Jefferson to Martha Jefferson Randolph, 3 July 1792," *Founders Online,* National Archives, last modified June 13, 2018, http://founders.archives.gov/documents/Jefferson/01-24-02-0160.

[71] "From Thomas Jefferson to Martha Jefferson Randolph, 13 July 1792," *Founders Online,* National Archives, last modified June 13, 2018, http://founders.archives.gov/documents/Jefferson/01-24-02-0215.

[72] "From Thomas Jefferson to Martha Jefferson Randolph, 26 October 1792," *Founders Online,* National Archives, last modified June 13, 2018, http://founders.archives.gov/documents/Jefferson/01-24-02-0490.

[73] "From Thomas Jefferson to Martha Jefferson Randolph, 12 November 1792," *Founders Online,* National Archives, last modified June 13, 2018, http://founders.archives.gov/documents/Jefferson/01-24-02-0579.

[74] "To Thomas Jefferson from Martha Jefferson Randolph, 18 November 1792," *Founders Online,* National Archives, last modified June 13, 2018, http://founders.archives.gov/documents/Jefferson/01-24-02-0613.

[75] "From Thomas Jefferson to Martha Jefferson Randolph, 22 November 1792," *Founders Online,* National Archives, last modified June 13, 2018, http://founders.archives.gov/documents/Jefferson/01-24-02-0638.

[76] "From Thomas Jefferson to Martha Jefferson Randolph, 6 December 1792," *Founders Online,* National Archives, last modified June 13, 2018, http://founders.archives.gov/documents/Jefferson/01-24-02-0692.

[77] "From Thomas Jefferson to Martha Jefferson Randolph, 13 December 1792," *Founders Online,* National Archives, last modified June 13, 2018, http://founders.archives.gov/documents/Jefferson/01-24-02-0723.

[78] "From Thomas Jefferson to Martha Jefferson Randolph, 31 December 1792," *Founders Online,* National Archives, last modified June 13, 2018, http://founders.archives.gov/documents/Jefferson/01-24-02-0782.

[79] "From Thomas Jefferson to Martha Jefferson Randolph, 14 January 1793," *Founders Online,* National Archives, last modified June 13, 2018, http://founders.archives.gov/documents/Jefferson/01-25-02-0056.

[80] "To Thomas Jefferson from Martha Jefferson Randolph, 16 January 1793," *Founders Online,* National Archives, last modified June 13, 2018, http://founders.archives.gov/documents/Jefferson/01-25-02-0074.

[81] "From Thomas Jefferson to Martha Jefferson Randolph, 26 January 1793," *Founders Online,* National Archives, last modified June 13, 2018, http://founders.archives.gov/documents/Jefferson/01-25-02-0103.

[82] "From Thomas Jefferson to Martha Jefferson Randolph, 11 February 1793," *Founders Online,* National Archives, last modified June 13, 2018, http://founders.archives.gov/documents/Jefferson/01-25-02-0160.

[83] "From Thomas Jefferson to Martha Jefferson Randolph, 24 February 1793," *Founders Online,* National Archives, last modified June 13, 2018, http://founders.archives.gov/documents/Jefferson/01-25-02-0233.

[84] "To Thomas Jefferson from Martha Jefferson Randolph, 27 February 1793," *Founders Online,* National Archives, last modified June 13, 2018, http://founders.archives.gov/documents/Jefferson/01-25-02-0261.

[85] "From Thomas Jefferson to Martha Jefferson Randolph, 10 March 1793," *Founders Online,* National Archives, last modified June 13, 2018, http://founders.archives.gov/documents/Jefferson/01-25-02-0314.

[86] "From Thomas Jefferson to Martha Jefferson Randolph, 24 March 1793," *Founders Online,* National Archives, last modified June 13, 2018, http://founders.archives.gov/documents/Jefferson/01-25-02-0410.

[87] "From Thomas Jefferson to Martha Jefferson Randolph, 8 April 1793," *Founders Online,* National Archives, last modified June 13, 2018, http://founders.archives.gov/documents/Jefferson/01-25-02-0479.

[88] "From Thomas Jefferson to Martha Jefferson Randolph, 28 April 1793," *Founders Online,* National Archives, last modified June 13, 2018, http://founders.archives.gov/documents/Jefferson/01-25-02-0566.

[89] "From Thomas Jefferson to Martha Jefferson Randolph, 12 May 1793," *Founders Online,* National Archives, last modified June 13, 2018, http://founders.archives.gov/documents/Jefferson/01-26-02-0014.

[90] "To Thomas Jefferson from Martha Jefferson Randolph, 16 May 1793," *Founders Online,* National Archives, last modified June 13, 2018, http://founders.archives.gov/documents/Jefferson/01-26-02-0042.

[91] "From Thomas Jefferson to Martha Jefferson Randolph, 26 May 1793," *Founders Online,* National Archives, last modified June 13, 2018, http://founders.archives.gov/documents/Jefferson/01-26-02-0115.

[92] "From Thomas Jefferson to Martha Jefferson Randolph, 10 June 1793," *Founders Online,* National Archives, last modified June 13, 2018, http://founders.archives.gov/documents/Jefferson/01-26-02-0226.

[93] "To Thomas Jefferson from Martha Jefferson Randolph, 26 June 1793," *Founders Online,* National Archives, last modified June 13, 2018, http://founders.archives.gov/documents/Jefferson/01-26-02-0344.

[94] "From Thomas Jefferson to Martha Jefferson Randolph, 7 July 1793," *Founders Online,* National Archives, last modified June 13, 2018, http://founders.archives.gov/documents/Jefferson/01-26-02-0394.

[95] "From Thomas Jefferson to Martha Jefferson Randolph, 21 July 1793," *Founders Online,* National Archives, last modified June 13, 2018, http://founders.archives.gov/documents/Jefferson/01-26-02-0481.

[96] "From Thomas Jefferson to Martha Jefferson Randolph, 4 August 1793," *Founders Online,* National Archives, last modified June 13, 2018, http://founders.archives.gov/documents/Jefferson/01-26-02-0558.

[97] "From Thomas Jefferson to Martha Jefferson Randolph, 18 August 1793," *Founders Online,* National Archives, last modified June 13, 2018, http://founders.archives.gov/documents/Jefferson/01-26-02-0638.

[98] "From Thomas Jefferson to Martha Jefferson Randolph, 8 September 1793," *Founders Online,* National Archives, last modified June 13, 2018, http://founders.archives.gov/documents/Jefferson/01-27-02-0060.

99] "From Thomas Jefferson to Martha Jefferson Randolph, 10 November 1793," *Founders Online,* National Archives, last modified June 3, 2018, http://founders.archives.gov/documents/Jefferson/ 01-27-02-0309.

100] "From Thomas Jefferson to Martha Jefferson Randolph, 1 December 1793," *Founders Online,* National Archives, last modified June 13, 2018, http://founders.archives.gov/documents/Jefferson/ 01-27-02-0437.

101] "From Thomas Jefferson to Martha Jefferson Randolph, 22 December 1793," *Founders Online,* National Archives, last modified June 13, 2018, http://founders.archives.gov/documents/Jefferson/ 01-27-02-0536.

102] "From Thomas Jefferson to Martha Jefferson Randolph, 27 March 1797," *Founders Online,* National Archives, last modified June 13, 2018, http://founders.archives.gov/documents/Jefferson/01-29-02-0260.

103] "To Thomas Jefferson from Martha Jefferson Randolph, 31 March 1797," *Founders Online,* National Archives, last modified June 13, 2018, http://founders.archives.gov/documents/Jefferson/01-29-02-0265.

104] "From Thomas Jefferson to Martha Jefferson Randolph, 9 April 1797," *Founders Online,* National Archives, last modified June 13, 2018, http://founders.archives.gov/documents/Jefferson/01-29-02-0274.

105] "From Thomas Jefferson to Martha Jefferson Randolph, 18 May 1797," *Founders Online,* National Archives, last modified June 13, 2018, http://founders.archives.gov/documents/Jefferson/01-29-02-0298.

[106] "From Thomas Jefferson to Martha Jefferson Randolph, 8 June 1797," *Founders Online,* National Archives, last modified June 13, 2018, http://founders.archives.gov/documents/Jefferson/01-29-02-0333.

[107] "From Thomas Jefferson to Martha Jefferson Randolph, 27 December 1797," *Founders Online,* National Archives, last modified June 13, 2018, http://founders.archives.gov/documents/Jefferson/ 01-29-02-0480.

[108] "To Thomas Jefferson from Martha Jefferson Randolph, 22 January 1798," *Founders Online,* National Archives, last modified June 13, 2018, http://founders.archives.gov/documents/Jefferson/01-30-02-0028.

[109] "From Thomas Jefferson to Martha Jefferson Randolph, 8 February 1798," *Founders Online,* National Archives, last modified June 13, 2018, http://founders.archives.gov/documents/Jefferson/01-30-02-0061.

[110] "To Thomas Jefferson from Martha Jefferson Randolph, 26 February 1798," *Founders Online,* National Archives, last modified June 13, 2018, http://founders.archives.gov/documents/Jefferson/01-30-02-0095.

[111] "From Thomas Jefferson to Martha Jefferson Randolph, 5 April 1798," *Founders Online,* National Archives, last modified June 13, 2018, http://founders.archives.gov/documents/Jefferson/01-30-02-0169.

[112] "To Thomas Jefferson from Martha Jefferson Randolph, 12 May 1798," *Founders Online,* National Archives, last modified June 13, 2018, http://founders.archives.gov/documents/Jefferson/01-30-02-0243.

[113] "From Thomas Jefferson to Martha Jefferson Randolph, 17 May 1798," *Founders Online,* National Archives, last modified June 13, 2018, http://founders.archives.gov/documents/Jefferson/01-30-02-0251.

[114] "From Thomas Jefferson to Martha Jefferson Randolph, 31 May 1798," *Founders Online,* National Archives, last modified June 13, 2018, http://founders.archives.gov/documents/Jefferson/01-30-02-0271.

[115] "From Thomas Jefferson to Martha Jefferson Randolph, 15 August 1798," *Founders Online,* National Archives, last modified June 13, 2018, http://founders.archives.gov/documents/Jefferson/01-30-02-0345.

[116] "From Thomas Jefferson to Martha Jefferson Randolph, 27 December 1798," *Founders Online,* National Archives, last modified June 13, 2018, http://founders.archives.gov/documents/Jefferson/01-30-02-0413.

[117] "From Thomas Jefferson to Martha Jefferson Randolph, 23 January 1799," *Founders Online,* National Archives, last modified June 13, 2018, http://founders.archives.gov/documents/Jefferson/01-30-02-0443.

[118] "From Thomas Jefferson to Martha Jefferson Randolph, 5 February 1799," *Founders Online,* National Archives, last modified June 13, 2018, http://founders.archives.gov/documents/Jefferson/01-31-02-0006.

[119] "To Thomas Jefferson from Martha Jefferson Randolph, 8 February 1799," *Founders Online,* National Archives, last modified June 13, 2018, http://founders.archives.gov/documents/Jefferson/01-31-02-0013.

[120] "To Thomas Jefferson from Martha Jefferson Randolph, 22 February 1799," *Founders Online,* National Archives, last modified June 13, 2018, http://founders.archives.gov/documents/Jefferson/01-31-02-0036.

[121] "From Thomas Jefferson to Martha Jefferson Randolph, 21 January 1800," *Founders Online,* National Archives, last modified June 13, 2018, http://founders.archives.gov/documents/Jefferson/01-31-02-0282.

[122] "To Thomas Jefferson from Martha Jefferson Randolph, 30 January 1800," *Founders Online,* National Archives, last modified June 13, 2018, http://founders.archives.gov/documents/Jefferson/01-31-02-0294.

[123] "From Thomas Jefferson to Martha Jefferson Randolph, 11 February 1800," *Founders Online,* National Archives, last modified June 13, 2018, http://founders.archives.gov/documents/Jefferson/01-31-02-0311.

[124] "From Thomas Jefferson to Martha Jefferson Randolph, 22 April 1800," *Founders Online,* National Archives, last modified June 13, 2018, http://founders.archives.gov/documents/Jefferson/01-31-02-0446.

[125] "To Thomas Jefferson from Martha Jefferson Randolph, 15 May 1800," *Founders Online,* National Archives, last modified June 13, 2018, http://founders.archives.gov/documents/Jefferson/01-31-02-0486.

[126] "From Thomas Jefferson to Martha Jefferson Randolph, 16 January 1801," *Founders Online,* National Archives, last modified June 13, 2018, http://founders.archives.gov/documents/Jefferson/01-32-02-0339.

[127] "To Thomas Jefferson from Martha Jefferson Randolph and Thomas Mann Randolph, 31 January 1801," *Founders Online,* National Archives, last modified June 13, 2018, http://founders.archives.gov/documents/Jefferson/01-32-02-0375.

[128] "From Thomas Jefferson to Martha Jefferson Randolph, 5 February 1801," *Founders Online,* National Archives, last modified June 13, 2018, http://founders.archives.gov/documents/Jefferson/01-32-02-0397.

[129] "From Thomas Jefferson to Martha Jefferson Randolph, 28 May 1801," *Founders Online,* National Archives, last modified June 13, 2018, http://founders.archives.gov/documents/Jefferson/01-34-02-0162.

[130] "To Thomas Jefferson from Martha Jefferson Randolph, 19 June 1801," *Founders Online,* National Archives, last modified June 13, 2018, http://founders.archives.gov/documents/Jefferson/01-34-02-0305.

[131] "From Thomas Jefferson to Martha Jefferson Randolph, 25 June 1801," *Founders Online,* National Archives, last modified June 13, 2018, http://founders.archives.gov/documents/Jefferson/01-34-02-0352.

[132] "From Thomas Jefferson to Martha Jefferson Randolph, 16 July 1801," *Founders Online,* National Archives, last modified June 13, 2018, http://founders.archives.gov/documents/Jefferson/01-34-02-0441.

[133] "To Thomas Jefferson from Martha Jefferson Randolph, 25 July 1801," *Founders Online,* National Archives, last modified June 13, 2018, http://founders.archives.gov/documents/Jefferson/01-34-02-0489.

[134] "From Thomas Jefferson to Martha Jefferson Randolph, 19 October 1801," *Founders Online,* National Archives, last modified June 13, 2018, http://founders.archives.gov/documents/Jefferson/01-35-02-0384.

[135] "To Thomas Jefferson from Martha Jefferson Randolph, 18 November 1801," *Founders Online,* National Archives, last modified June 13, 2018, http://founders.archives.gov/documents/Jefferson/01-35-02-0528.

[136] "From Thomas Jefferson to Martha Jefferson Randolph, 27 November 1801," *Founders Online,* National Archives, last modified June 13, 2018, http://founders.archives.gov/documents/Jefferson/01-35-02-0562.

[137] "From Thomas Jefferson to Martha Jefferson Randolph, 17 January 1802," *Founders Online,* National Archives, last modified June 13, 2018, http://founders.archives.gov/documents/Jefferson/01-36-02-0240.

[138] "From Thomas Jefferson to Martha Jefferson Randolph, 3 April 1802," *Founders Online,* National Archives, last modified June 13, 2018, http://founders.archives.gov/documents/Jefferson/01-37-02-0149.

[139] "To Thomas Jefferson from Martha Jefferson Randolph, 16 April 1802," *Founders Online,* National Archives, last modified June 13, 2018, http://founders.archives.gov/documents/Jefferson/01-37-02-0208.

[140] "From Thomas Jefferson to Martha Jefferson Randolph, 24 April 1802," *Founders Online,* National Archives, last modified June 13, 2018, http://founders.archives.gov/documents/Jefferson/01-37-02-0260.

[141] "From Thomas Jefferson to Martha Jefferson Randolph, 3 June 1802," *Founders Online,* National Archives, last modified June 13, 2018, http://founders.archives.gov/documents/Jefferson/01-37-02-0432-0001.

[142] "From Thomas Jefferson to Martha Jefferson Randolph, 18 June 1802," *Founders Online,* National Archives, last modified June 13, 2018, http://founders.archives.gov/documents/Jefferson/01-37-02-0509.

[143] "From Thomas Jefferson to Martha Jefferson Randolph, 2 July 1802," *Founders Online,* National Archives, last modified June 13, 2018, http://founders.archives.gov/documents/Jefferson/01-38-02-0013.

[144] "To Thomas Jefferson from Martha Jefferson Randolph, 10 July 1802," *Founders Online,* National Archives, last modified June 13, 2018, http://founders.archives.gov/documents/Jefferson/01-38-02-0047.

[145] "From Thomas Jefferson to Martha Jefferson Randolph, 7 October 1802," *Founders Online,* National Archives, last modified June 13, 2018, http://founders.archives.gov/documents/Jefferson/01-38-02-0420.

[146] "From Thomas Jefferson to Martha Jefferson Randolph, 18 October 1802," *Founders Online,* National Archives, last modified June 13, 2018, http://founders.archives.gov/documents/Jefferson/01-38-02-0482.

[147] "To Thomas Jefferson from Martha Jefferson Randolph, 29 October 1802," *Founders Online,* National Archives, last modified June 13, 2018, http://founders.archives.gov/documents/Jefferson/01-38-02-0537.

[148] "From Thomas Jefferson to Martha Jefferson Randolph, 2 November 1802," *Founders Online,* National Archives, last modified June 13, 2018, http://founders.archives.gov/documents/Jefferson/01-38-02-0557.

[149] "To Thomas Jefferson from Martha Jefferson Randolph, 9 November 1802," *Founders Online,* National Archives, last modified June 13, 2018, http://founders.archives.gov/documents/Jefferson/01-38-02-0584.

[150] "From Thomas Jefferson to Martha Jefferson Randolph, 27 January 1803," *Founders Online,* National Archives, last modified June 13, 2018, http://founders.archives.gov/documents/Jefferson/01-39-02-0349.

[151] "From Thomas Jefferson to Martha Jefferson Randolph, 25 April 1803," *Founders Online,* National Archives, last modified June 13, 2018, http://founders.archives.gov/documents/Jefferson/01-40-02-0198.

[152] "From Thomas Jefferson to Martha Jefferson Randolph, 7 November 1803," *Founders Online,* National Archives, last modified June 13, 2018, http://founders.archives.gov/documents/Jefferson/01-41-02-0507.

[153] "From Thomas Jefferson to Martha Jefferson Randolph, 23 January 1804," *Founders Online,* National Archives, last modified June 13, 2018, http://founders.archives.gov/documents/Jefferson/01-42-02-0290.

[154] "From Thomas Jefferson to Martha Jefferson Randolph, 8 March 1804," *Founders Online,* National Archives, last modified June 13, 2018, http://founders.archives.gov/documents/Jefferson/01-42-02-0532.

Authors Bio

Hello! I'm a native Minnesotan, who loves to read and write books. Among other things I love to watch movies and to hang out with my friends. My profile pic is of a squirrel that bit me in Washington D.C.

Made in the USA
Middletown, DE
31 May 2021